TAKE
A BISHOP
LIKE ME

TAKE A BISHOP LIKE ME

Paul Moore, Jr.

Harper & Row, Publishers
New York, Hagerstown, San Francisco, London

For Brenda

FIRST EDITION

Designed by Janice Stern

Library of Congress Cataloging in Publication Data

Moore, Paul, Jr. Date
    Take a Bishop like me.
    1. Ordination of women—Protestant Episcopal Church in the U.S.A.
2. Protestant Episcopal Church in the U.S.A.—Clergy. 3. Homosexuality and Christianity. 4. Moore, Paul, Jr.   I. Title.
BX5695.M66
1979   253'.2   78–2148
ISBN 0–06–013018–0

---

79 80 81 82 83 10 9 8 7 6 5 4 3 2 1

Contents

Preface

Can women be priests? Can homosexuals of either sex be priests? Both these questions excite delicate and sometimes dangerous religious and sexual emotions because their answers require a reexamination of the very meaning of human sexuality.

Recently these questions were asked and answered within a relatively small institution, the Episcopal Church in the United States. It is, however, in such small settings that great changes in society can begin. This is the story of my own involvement with these questions, where and how they were resolved, and the people around whom the issues and answers formed themselves.

Few realize the heartbreak and tragedy undergone by homosexual persons because of the misunderstanding, fear, and anger many people have for them. Few talk openly with gay persons about their sexuality. It is easy, then, for most of us to dismiss "them" as a category of undesirables, instead of acknowledging that they include our brothers, sisters, parents, children, indeed, ourselves. It is also true that few realize the devastating effect of the cosmic male chauvinism in the Judeo-Christian tradition; how it has not only distorted our view of women on the deepest level, but has also distorted our view of God.

Throughout the struggle for civil rights in the last decades,

I thought that I had seen firsthand the worst of any prejudice grounded in emotion. But the swirl of outrage and prejudice I encountered in 1977, when I ordained a qualified woman to the priesthood who had acknowledged publicly that she had homosexual tendencies, was far more devastating to me. My mail included more than one thousand letters in three months, with seventy-five percent of them against the ordination. Furthermore, there was a motion in the American House of Bishops to censure me.

First I wanted to publish a collection of these most revealing letters. Some were touching letters from gay persons, their friends and families. Others were angry and outraged. As I began to assemble them and reread them I was struck by two things: first, that human sexuality was something most people were afraid of; second, that there was real questioning going on among people who were unsatisfied with our society's present inconsistent and hypocritical views of sexuality. Reading other people's experiences made me think about my past and how my own views had been formed. Before long this book began to take shape.

I am indebted to the Reverend Richard Norris, Professor of Theology at Union Theological Seminary in New York, who advised me theologically but who has no responsibility for the views expressed. A legal and discerning eye was cast over the manuscript by my old friend, Robert Potter. Ms. Thelma Pyle typed and retyped chapters with style and understanding. I am enormously grateful to Ellen Barrett, who has continued her vocation with dignity and courage and has graciously allowed me to write about her.

Finally, I would like to acknowledge the generosity of spirit shown by the late Right Reverend Harold L. Wright, who was immediately responsible for the screening and training of candidates for ministry in this diocese. Although he differed with me on many issues, he maintained strong loyalty and gave me moral support throughout. He died suddenly on June 11, 1978.

Prologue

December 1974. Silence in the great cathedral. I sat in my bishop's chair, the eyes of the congregation upon me. A moment ago, my hands, the bishop's hands, had been placed on the heads of five men and the solemn words pronounced: "Receive the Holy Ghost for the Office and Work of a Priest in the Church of God, now committed unto thee by the imposition of our hands. Whose sins thou dost forgive they are forgiven; whose sins thou dost retain, they are retained. And be thou a faithful Dispenser of the Word of God, and of his holy Sacraments; in the Name of the Father, and of the Son, and of the Holy Ghost. Amen."

A movement caught my eye, and as I looked to the left I saw the women deacons of our diocese approaching. This was not part of the planned liturgy. They had had a part earlier in the service. One of them had read a statement of protest; and I had joined the protest in my sermon, decrying sexism in the Church. But now we were supposed to go forward with the ordination Eucharist. What was going on? Did the women deacons have their signals crossed? I looked helplessly to the master of ceremonies, under whose firm hand for the last thirty years archbishops, boy scouts, funeral corteges, and even kings and queens had moved without a whimper.

For once in his life, he did not have the situation under

1

control. His face was aghast as the women processed toward the space before the bishop's throne. There they stopped, knelt down, and looked up to me with what seemed the pain of a thousand years. They looked up and offered to their bishop their vocation to the office of priest. I knew them, each of them. I knew Julia, who spent her days at the bedside of the dying in Cancer Memorial Hospital. I knew Carter, who was turned down as a deacon by another bishop. In New York she had assumed the leadership of the women's cause. I knew Barbara and had shared with her the excitement of teaching in her school. And Carol, tall, commanding, beautiful, who by her ministry had won majority support from one of New York's most sophisticated parishes for women's ordination to the priesthood. There was Emily, a theologian soon to attend Harvard Law School. Each one had worked beyond the demands of her vocation. Each had suffered. Each had passed all the qualifications and screening necessary to be ordained a "priest in the Church of God." My hands involuntarily began to move forward to lay upon their heads, upon their lives, the burden and glory of priesthood. I knew I could not; yet in that moment, as the congregation gasped and leaned forward in their seats, a holy silence made all of us aware of the presence of God. The congregation, the women deacons, and even I wondered whether my hands would resist.

In the distance a siren sounded the life of the city outside. The spell was broken. I arose and began the Creed: "I believe in God, the Father Almighty, maker of heaven and earth . . . " I saw the women, who were my friends, get up from their knees. The hope in their eyes clouded into hurt and anger. They turned and walked down the aisle and out of the cathedral.

So much had brought us to that day, so much would follow. For around this struggle within a small denomination, a tiny fraction of Christendom, swirled the deepest feelings of mankind, thousands of years of history, the understanding of priesthood, of the nature of human sexuality, indeed of the very nature of God.

December 1975. Another ordination took place on a winter evening one month later; not in a cathedral this time, but in an old stone church on West Twentieth Street in New York City. I love St. Peter's, Chelsea. Years ago, its rector had written "The Night Before Christmas," and it was the parish where I had first worked for the Church as a seminarian. There I had played with the children on the streets and had learned a little of what life was like in the inner city.

There were less than sixty people in the church that winter evening: old ladies who had been members of St. Peter's for years, a few neighborhood kids, and some of the faculty from a nearby seminary. The unusual thing about this ordination was that the young woman soon to be a deacon and later a priest had declared herself to be homosexual. Several years before, she had joined a small group of Episcopalians in forming Integrity, a gay fellowship that had the courage to be open about homosexuality.

The service was quiet but filled with warmth. The congregation knew what was at stake. Other members of Integrity were there, and Ellen Barrett's mother stood in the front pew with all the dignity of a Southern lady. In my sermon I spoke about the role of a deacon in the Church. This order of ministry has always been associated with *diakonos,* service in the name of the humble Christ who washed the disciples' feet the night before He died. The liturgy began. When we came to that part of the service where objections can be raised, no one stood up. With a sense of relief, I proceeded. When Ellen knelt before me, it seemed right that this quiet, honest, courageous woman should put on the deacon's stole.

The Eucharist that followed drew together in unity that strangely mixed congregation. I had no idea, that night, where this ordination would lead.

The women's movement, as so often happens with movements indirectly nurtured by Christian thought and experience, had come back fresh and vigorous to challenge the very Church from whose teaching it was born. This movement for women's identity had encouraged an even more complicated struggle, that of gay liberation. Nor can these movements be separated from the current conflict over abortion, or indeed, from our whole understanding of human sexuality.

Bishops, who are believed to be successors of the apostles, must deal with issues such as these. They are called to be prophets of truth prevailing over social injustice, and conservators of virtue against the licentiousness of secular society. The office demands an acting out, by word and deed, of the love of God appropriate to their time and place. Bishops are mandated to preserve the unity, health, and growth of the Church. They are the healers, the reconcilers, the pastors. They are preachers of the Word of God, not "man-pleasers." They occupy the center of the institutional life of the strangest of all institutions, the Church.

Whatever bishops are said to be in the doctrine of the Church, whatever they are supposed to be in the tradition of the church, whatever different people expect them to be, each bishop is a human being, formed by his own background and experience.

Take a bishop like me. How would I respond to the issues which came before the Church in New York in the 1970s?

1

I Love New York

My first memories of New York were clothed in a child's imagination. We lived in the country in Morristown, New Jersey, and I never "went to town" when I was a child. But I heard my parents talk about New York. I imagined a dark, mysterious place that only grown-ups were allowed to enter. When I did finally go, the trip was very, very long, or so it seemed. We drove through villages and towns on the way: Madison, Chatham, Summit, the Oranges (I kept looking for oranges and none were there), through Newark and across the flats. In those days the smell of the pig farms of Hohokus enveloped the misty atmosphere of the marshes on either side of the cobblestone road. Then came Hoboken and the ferry. The ferry terminal looked like a green castle built for a river king. It opened up to us, and we drove across a moat on worn beams and entered the dark hold where sea and oil and gasoline smells mixed together. It was a great thrill to climb up to the deck, to see the Woolworth building, the tallest building in the world, and the Statue of Liberty in the distance. After we crossed the river, I felt the delicious crunch of the ferry's snub nose bumping into the piling walls until we were lined up just right.

We would stay at my grandmother's house on East Fifty-fourth Street. Four East Fifty-four . . . Granny in New York . . . strange to see her there, because I knew her best at the seashore. There was an elevator in the house and a pool table and a real lion made into a rug. At night I could hear the traffic's low roar and I snuggled into the great big bed and said to myself, "I'm in New York."

I had a protected youth, free from any hardship, given all I needed and much more: a dog, a bicycle, a pony. I was protected from even seeing poverty. But I do remember once driving through Hoboken in a fancy car during the Depression and being so embarrassed by my opulence that when we passed the bread lines I hid on the floor of the car.

I attended a church school, St. Paul's, in New Hampshire, where the students were from families like mine, but where the living conditions were self-consciously austere. It was during my senior year that I experienced a religious conversion when I made my first confession. I went to Yale, of course, because my father and my uncles and my brother and my ever-so-great grandfather went to Yale. I enjoyed college life, and lived it to the full: friends, athletics, parties, drinking, studying hard. I also continued an active life of prayer and service in the community. I remember having to take a boy scout troop to inspect an undertaker's establishment.

After graduation I entered the Marine Corps and was wounded at Guadalcanal. I was in combat only three months, but the experience deepened my understanding of sacrifice and courage, of brutality and cowardice, of endurance and death. I was an enthusiastic Marine and loved the men in my platoon. Seven of them were killed before my eyes. I myself almost died on the battlefield. I came home deeply shaken, but even more certain of my faith. When the peace came, I had already decided to go to seminary.

I was married to Jenny McKean in 1944 and we had one daughter, with plans for many more children. The seminary, in the Chelsea section of New York, was stimulating academi-

cally and set in the middle of what was then a poor neighborhood. Two of the junior faculty, my wife, and I worked at
a nearby church, St. Peter's, and became committed to an
inner-city ministry. I loved the neighborhood kids. They were
tough, bright, alert, funny. They reminded me of my Marines.
I loved walking the sidewalks and climbing dark, smelly tene-
ment stairs to knock on strange doors where the children
lived. It made me feel I was following in the footsteps of
the great London priests of the turn of the century who had
inspired me so long ago when I read about them at school.
I suppose I felt guilty about the rich upbringing I had been
given, I may have had a martyr complex; I am sure I felt
holier than thou but was much too holy to admit it! Whatever
the mixed motives, this ministry seemed real and made my
prayers, the Communion service, the Bible, and indeed Jesus
Himself come alive in a way that the classes at seminary and
the beautiful Evensong in the chapel never had.

From that time on, I was drawn to the cause of the poor
and the persecuted in a special way. We moved to Jersey
City and continued this ministry not far from the Hoboken
through which I was driven in a fancy car twenty-five years
before. We lived there and tried to tackle as best we could
the massive burdens of the slums, as they still were called.
In those early days of the civil rights movement, I joined
the local National Association for the Advancement of Colored People and in 1950 accompanied Thurgood Marshall,
now a Supreme Court Justice, on the investigation of a rape
case in Groveland, Florida. I was amazed by what we saw
in that Florida town. I did not expect such violence and brutality in America. I was even more amazed when our lives
were threatened and we were forced to leave town.

After eight years in Jersey City, it was time to move on.
In 1957 I accepted a call to become dean of Christ Church
Cathedral in Indianapolis. This ministry was far more compli-
cated than in Jersey City. We had resources, a position of

respect in the community, but in Indianapolis, social action and racial integration were suspect. My goals were the same, but the action slowed down. We had our last two children there. Now the family numbered six girls and three boys.

In 1964 I was elected suffragan bishop of the Diocese of Washington. Shortly after I arrived, the civil rights struggle reached a new intensity. I was involved in the local problems of black people in Washington. Dr. Martin Luther King and I led a march to the White House to dramatize the need for home rule for the District of Columbia, I registered voters in Mississippi, and in both places my life was threatened.

When the civil rights movement was taken over by black leadership and the role of white persons within it virtually ceased to exist, I turned to the peace movement, which was beginning to gain momentum. The year 1970 found me in Vietnam on a mission to the Vietnamese underground peace group. My visit ended by being tear-gassed outside the United States Embassy. When I returned I received a long letter from my former Marine battalion commander, then commanding general of the Marines in Vietnam. He could not understand how a good Marine could have done such a thing. It was strange to recall, as I saw the Vietnamese soldiers fire off their tear gas grenades, that the last time a grenade was lobbed over my head was when I was swimming across a river in the Solomon Islands almost thirty years before. Inconsistent? Perhaps, but both times I felt I was fighting for freedom, peace, and the dignity of the individual.

World War II, civil rights for blacks, peace, and now the most unlikely of all causes for an old Marine to be involved in, the women's movement. I recall being first conscious of women's issues when my wife read Simone de Beauvoir's *The Second Sex,* long before there was a visible movement. But gradually the talk about it increased and the literature proliferated. James A. Pike, Bishop of California, caused the first debate on the subject in the House of Bishops in the mid-sixties. In 1970 the issue of ordaining women came before the Episcopal Church General Convention for the first time. When permission to ordain women priests was defeated a second time in 1973, the women's movement within the Church was going strong.

I came to New York as bishop coadjutor (assistant bishop with right of succession) in 1970, and became diocesan bishop in 1972. Given the nature of New York, I suppose it is not surprising that the women's movement, and the gay rights movement that followed, developed great strength there.

The Diocese of New York stretches from Staten Island to Tivoli, north of Poughkeepsie; from South Salem on the boundary of Connecticut to Callicoon, deep in the Catskills. There are two hundred parish churches within the diocese.

Staten Island parishes, some dating from before the Revolution, tend to be fairly conservative, the parishioners resentful toward the newcomers from Brooklyn who have moved there since the building of the Verrazano Bridge. At the tip of Manhattan, historic Trinity Church stands at the head of Wall Street. Although hard hit by recent economic trends, it is still the richest parish in the country. The nearby Chapel of St. Paul, the only church visible from City Hall, has a pew where George Washington worshiped. Not far uptown on the East Side is a mission to Chinatown, and north of that, a parish of Lower East Side blacks and Hispanics.

Greenwich Village has five parishes, each with its own personality. St. Mark's in the Bowery, recently severely damaged by fire, is surrounded by a cemetery where Peter Stuyvesant, the last Dutch governor of New York, is buried. The cemetery has been relandscaped by a group of young Puerto Ricans who talk about Marxism and Christianity with their Hispanic rector. Near Times Square, old St. Clement's doubles as a theater. When you visit there on Sunday, you worship on

the set of their latest off-Broadway play. One year, I confirmed new members of the church in a junkyard.

Not far from there, on Fifth Avenue, is the beautiful Gothic
church of St. Thomas, to which my grandmother walked on
Sunday mornings from her house on Fifty-fourth Street. Far-
ther east, St. Bartholomew's, the largest Episcopal parish
church in Manhattan, stands next to the Waldorf-Astoria Hotel. On the West Side is St. Ann's Church for the Deaf, run
by a woman priest who is also a nun, and in the same building,
a Haitian congregation where I attempt to read the service
in French.

Overlooking Harlem from Morningside Heights is the
Cathedral of St. John the Divine, the largest cathedral in
the world, eclectic, unfinished, dirty on the outside and im-
mensely powerful within. I live with my family on one floor
of a French-style château built as the residence of the Bishop
of New York by J. P. Morgan on the cathedral grounds. When
asked, in 1912, why he had erected such a mansion for the
bishop, Morgan snorted: "He has a right to live like all the
rest of us!" There is also a school on the Cathedral Close,
as well as the diocesan headquarters building, offices for
housing programs, and so forth. The cathedral ministers to
many different groups, including Sufis, and is used for a variety of activities, even the Big Apple Circus School.

North of the cathedral, in Harlem itself, are many of the
largest and most active parishes in the diocese, the oldest
of which, St. Philip's, is venerated by black Episcopalians
throughout the Church. St. Philip's has recently built several
large housing developments for the elderly and a new community center. West Indians, brought up strong Anglicans
at home in the islands, form the backbone of the Church's
strength in New York. We have many churches in the Bronx,
one of which houses the remains of Gouverneur Morris; the
beautiful colonial structure of this church is now situated
in the midst of a burnt-out barrio.

Westchester has wealthy suburban parishes, and there are inner-city churches in places like Yonkers, New Rochelle, Port Chester, and White Plains. The diocese flanks the Hudson with one or two churches in every river town. Throughout the rural areas are small churches, some of which have only a handful of people who worship on Sunday morning, but these old-time Episcopalians are loyal and passionate about their church. Other parishes, such as Hyde Park, where Franklin Roosevelt was senior warden, are flourishing.

Besides parishes, many institutions come under the direction of the bishop: the Episcopal Mission Society, which supervises institutional chaplains and runs centers for children; St. Luke's Hospital, independent administratively, yet strongly Episcopal; four religious orders watched over directly by the bishop, and several others functioning within the diocese; homes for the aged; centers for health-care and welfare administration.

The diocese is an enormous, loosely federated conglomerate, fascinating to be a part of, but frustrating to run, because a bishop in our Church has great status but little direct authority.

I am told that I was elected bishop because I was thought to be a strong Catholic churchman, a social activist, and because I knew many well-placed New Yorkers, and had helped revive interest in the work of the Church in the cities. I was thrilled when I heard that I had been elected on the second ballot, with enthusiasm. I had always hoped to return to New York, my favorite place in the world. To be the Bishop of New York seemed a God-sent opportunity to carry out ideas for urban mission, to use every bit of experience and energy I had, to finish my career in the Church with a tough and important assignment.

My first three years were extremely difficult and full of sorrow. My wife had a serious automobile accident soon after my election. She never really recovered, and after living in

New York for a year she had an emotional breakdown and had to move back to Washington to recover her equilibrium. The children moved with her, and I lived alone in my apartment in the Morgan château, not a very cheery existence. I commuted to Washington two days a week and tried to put on a brave front as I went about the diocese. I often wondered if I should resign, if I had somehow tempted the fates in accepting election, yielding, perhaps, to ambition at the expense of my family. I worried whether Jenny would ever be able to return to New York, and whether I was losing my children. In 1972 The Right Reverend Horace W. B. Donegan, my predecessor as Bishop, resigned, and in a great medieval ceremony at the cathedral I was installed as the thirteenth Bishop of New York. Thirteenth indeed!

I adjusted to my strange life style, and began to assume leadership in the diocese. I emphasized community responsibility and fund raising by the parishes and pushed various social issues. Occasionally I caused a stir. But by and large, things went well. I was out in the diocese as much as possible, especially in the northern areas, which tend to feel neglected because of their location. I came to know my clergy, began to unravel the mysteries of New York, and in general was beginning to be self-confident.

In the spring of 1973, Jenny and I took a long weekend in the country. The first night, she had a severe stomach disorder and was not able to sleep. We sat up most of the night talking about the future. She was worse in the morning, went to the hospital for tests, and was diagnosed as having a large tumor. They operated. It was cancer. She died in October 1973. Those were terrible months. I took a leave of absence and moved to Washington until the end.

My two youngest girls, Patience and Susanna, and I moved back to New York and tried to rebuild our lives in the gloomy old château. Two other children stayed in Washington. The rest were away and on their own. Gradually life began to make sense again, and the work of the diocese went forward. But I will never forget the terrible, sleepless nights when I wondered whether to resign, move back to Washington and bring up the children in their familiar surroundings, or to uproot them and trust in their resiliency. They showed great courage, and supported me in my decision to stay in New York.

My personal troubles drew many of the people in the diocese close to me. They were extraordinarily understanding and sympathetic. I made many close friends. The diocese in a sense had become my family, and my affection for its clergy and people went very deep.

About this time a friend of mine was diagnosed as having cancer. I was with him and his wife, Brenda, a good deal toward the end. After he died, I continued to see Brenda and my life came alive again. We were married by Canon Edward N. West in the spring of 1975, in the Bishop's Garden on the Cathedral Close.

The diocese was changing. A process of decentralization, begun just before I arrived, was completed at the end of 1973. The new plan divided the diocese into three regions: New York City, Westchester and Rockland counties, and northern counties. They now had more control over the use of their funds and a sense of geographical identity. It was a time of endless organizational meetings and administrative debate. By 1974 we were ready for some peace and quiet, but the great debate on the ordination of women was upon us. Furthermore, the economic slump in 1974 hit New York so severely that we have not recovered even now. The great, endowed parishes had less to give for mission, and costs of utilities and maintenance for the hundreds of old buildings used up the little margin the average parish had in its operating budget. Furthermore, the city was cutting back its public assistance programs, many of which were housed in church buildings, thereby helping to offset overhead costs.

We had some money in reserve, but it was fast running out. Many of our clergy were anxious and insecure about their jobs. Parishes were cutting back on their staffs. This was the climate when the controversies over women's ordination and the ordination of homosexuals broke open. I was a bishop in fairly good touch with his people, but with a diocese facing financial trouble. I had been Diocesan Bishop of New York for two years.

2

Are They Truly Called?

July 1974. The dying beauty of Venice was drawing me into a dream of history, the unreality of other times. The Cathedral of San Marco is a fantasy of churchliness . . . soaring angels, stamping horses, image after image of other worlds. My three youngest daughters and I left the cathedral and walked the hot distance across the square and through humid alleys to our hotel. Inside the stone doorway the concierge called my name. I was given a telegram: "Call Bishop DeWitt. Urgent."

"My Lord, what has that impulsive guy done now," I thought. When I heard his laconic Midwestern voice on the telephone I was yanked forcibly away from history, canals, and palaces to the realities of the Episcopal Church. "Paul," he said, "I just wanted you to know what we are planning to do on Monday. Dan Corrigan, Ed Welles, and I are going to ordain eleven women to the priesthood. Three of them are from your diocese: Carter, Emily, and Marie."

"DeWitt, you are out of your mind!" I said.

"The ordination is to take place in Philadelphia, at the Church of the Advocate," he added. This was a grand old cathedral-like structure now in the center of Philadelphia's ghetto, where the rector, a black priest, was known for his militancy.

"But, Bob, I thought we had agreed at that meeting where

15

the women walked out, just two months ago, that we were *not* going to ordain any women until after General Convention."

"Well," he said, "we have been meeting with some of the women and I think the only way is to just do it. We all agree that the canons are vague and . . . "

"But, Bob," I said, "it's all very well for you and Dan and Ed . . . you're retired or resigned from your dioceses, but it will leave the rest of us out on a limb. The Church will go around the bend and its whole machinery will be turned against us. You've double-crossed me."

Bob DeWitt was an old and close friend. We had been through many battles together. He had recently resigned as Bishop of Pennsylvania to put his full time into the social concerns of the Church. I trusted him. I liked his way of going ahead, if he felt he was right, whatever the consequences. This was the first time we had really differed. I was angry and hurt and feeling very, very far away.

"I'm sorry you feel like that, Paul. I can understand it. But the plans are set for Monday, and we did want you to know about them."

"Thanks a lot, Bob. . . . Well, I'm mad as hell about it but I guess there is nothing I can do. Keep me posted. Good luck."

The ordination took place. It clearly broke the canons because, apart from the question of the ordinands being women, they had not been approved by their own bishops and Standing Committees, nor had the three ordaining bishops received permission from the Bishop of Pennsylvania to function in his diocese.

The service took place with all the excitement and publicity attending an historic event. The Holy Spirit was felt to be there, the participants said. Statements of opposition were read. Television spread the story across the country.

The new Presiding Bishop of the national Episcopal

Church, who had been installed only that past June, quickly called a special meeting of the House of Bishops to deal with the illegal ordination. We were to meet at a motel at the Chicago airport for a day in the beginning of August 1974.

I have always felt that the atmosphere of a place affects the dynamics of any meeting; the atmosphere of the airport motel at O'Hare was bad. From the time we arrived until the time we went home we never went outside. It was a hot day and the air conditioning was on full blast. We were hermetically sealed from the world. As I entered the lobby I saw bishops lined up at the desk, bishops in knots of conversation by plastic potted palms, bishops greeting each other with more enthusiasm than they could possibly have felt. August is the time when almost every one of us can get away to be with our families. We had come to Chicago from Montana ranches, from Martha's Vineyard, from Florida beaches. One bishop was reached on a boat, another on a mountaintop. We were all irritated that the ordination had taken place. Those who favored women's ordination were upset that they were now on the defensive. We were working hard for proper legislation at the 1976 General Convention; we were working against two thousand years of tradition, and against explosive feelings. Now we were in a position where we either had to defend a basically illegal action or turn against three bishops and eleven women who were in the leadership of this movement. Those who were against women's ordination now had a "scandalous," uncanonical action to make them even more embittered. And no one knew how the new Presiding Bishop would chair a meeting.

The Most Reverend John Allin had been the Bishop of Mississippi during the 1960s. He had seen his mission during those days as one of reconciliation between the people of his diocese and the civil rights movement which invaded the

state of Mississippi during the "long hot summer" of 1964.
I was one of the many Northern clergy who had spent time
there. I had been with people who had been injured for
helping the movement, and others who had been killed. We
had slept in bombed-out houses, been chased in cars by angry
whites, and encountered oppression which seemed close to
that of Nazi Germany. Those of us who went to Mississippi
felt certain that we were doing the right thing, that we were
part of an historic movement of liberation. We had no patience with the feelings of the local Episcopalians. You were
either with us or against us. You were either a good guy
or a bad guy. Looking back on it, despite the righteousness
of the cause and the permanent liberating effect it had on
race relations in the South, I realize that we were self-righteous, and I can well understand the feelings of moderates
like Jack Allin. Over the years he had been trying to change
attitudes in a peaceful way and at the same time preserve
the life of the Church.

In the fall of 1964 I had been named chairman of the
Delta Ministry, an effort by the National Council of Churches
to continue a ministry of social service and political action
after the excitement of that "long hot summer" had subsided.
Thus an Episcopal bishop was holding a position of responsibility for an ecumenical operation within the jurisdiction of
another Episcopal bishop, which was not an easy situation
given the volatile dynamics of the sixties. Bishop Allin and
I were on a collision course and barely managed to maintain
even a strained relationship.

Who would have imagined in the mid-1960s that the
Bishop of Mississippi would become the Presiding Bishop
of the Episcopal Church? And yet, only nine years later, he
was elected by a coalition of theologically conservative Western bishops and socially conservative Southern bishops, who
had the election votes lined up even before the 1973 General
Convention opened.

Bishop Allin rightly sensed a division in the Church. He was elected by those who wished to slow the pace of change, but he was also aware of the many who wanted our Church to continue its leadership for social justice and for liturgical change. He wanted to continue on a national level the ministry of reconciliation he had begun in Mississippi. My hunch is that, if left alone, he would not have called this special meeting in Chicago. But, as I understand it, he was counseled otherwise. He was persuaded that this was his first leadership challenge and that he had to assert the order and discipline of the Church by bringing the matter before the House of Bishops. It was said their regular meeting in the fall would be too late. And so, for the first time in memory, a special meeting of the House of Bishops was called to confront a crisis.

The Episcopal Church is governed by a bicameral convention meeting every three years. Many of the same men who drafted the Constitution of the United States also drafted the Constitution of the Episcopal Church. The House of Bishops is analogous to the Senate. The House of Clerical (ordained) and Lay Deputies, elected from each diocese, is the equivalent of the House of Representatives. The Presiding Bishop runs the administration of the national Church between conventions, and is roughly equivalent to the President. The Church constitution also provides for an ecclesiastical system of courts (which has seldom been used and whose procedures are creaky, to say the least). Thus a meeting of the House of Bishops alone cannot pass canon law or exert judicial discipline. It can, however, make decisions about its own purview, about the official relationships between bishops, and can exert moral pressure when it speaks out formally.

To continue the parallel, each diocese is the equivalent of a state. Some, like Wyoming, are coterminous geographically with the state; other states, like New York, have several dioceses within them. Each diocese has its own legislative process called a diocesan convention; its own administration, the diocesan bishop and diocesan council; and a quasi-judiciary body elected from the diocesan convention and composed of four clergy and four lay persons, called the Standing Committee. Ecclesiastical courts are also available on that level. Each parish is an independent corporation governed by the rector and vestry, the latter elected at an annual parish meeting.

Thus the Episcopal Church functions as a constitutional democracy on the level of national church, diocese, and parish, with a carefully arranged balance of power between the clergy and the laity and between the various levels of jurisdiction. The national canon law, as in our secular government, takes precedence over the diocesan canon law, which in turn takes precedence over the bylaws of the parish.

The bishops in that Chicago airport motel ranged in age from early forties to retired bishops in their eighties. Each represented a different constituency, and having been elected by that constituency was likely to represent its views. Some bishops were scholars and seminary professors, others had come up through the parish ministry. Each had to go home and deal with the consequences of the House's action among his own people. And although a diocesan bishop (the head bishop of a diocese) and suffragan and coadjutor bishops (assistant bishops) are elected for life until retirement, nonetheless the smooth functioning and financial health of a diocese depend on the people's support of the bishop. In other words, much was at stake there for each one of us, both deeply held principles and administrative realities.

In calmer times the meetings of the House of Bishops were marked by great camaraderie. Differences were submerged beneath the collegiality of the House. One was reminded of the clubby atmosphere of the Senate. Friendships from seminary, common burdens, years of working together all tend to unite the bishops of the Church. In recent years, however, the stresses of the sixties have strained the fellowship, and political groupings have become more pronounced.

The Southern bishops, for instance, tended to vote as a bloc on social issues. The bishops from traditionally "High Church" dioceses were conservative in theological and liturgical matters. The bishops from the East and West Coasts were rather liberal in both social and theological matters, whether they had grown up in Low Church (more Protestant in emphasis) or High Church (more Catholic in emphasis) traditions. The liberals had been in the ascendancy in the 1960s, but by this time, as in the society in general, conservatives were regaining their strength.

Of course, group labels are less than accurate. From time to time individuals will vote differently from accustomed patterns. Each bishop examines his own conscience and faith thoroughly before making up his mind. The issue of women's ordination elicited such divergent responses. For instance, the Bishop of California, a leader in the civil rights movement, initially came out strongly against the ordination of women. One or two conservatives felt strongly in favor. However, all of us were perplexed by the problems of the illegal ordinations in Philadelphia.

That August morning, we crowded into a private meeting room, nervous, uncertain, not knowing how our colleagues felt. The Presiding Bishop called us to order and we stood for the opening prayers, urgently asking God's help for the Church, for this meeting, and for our own role within it. The three bishops who had ordained the women illegally sat together on the left. They seemed like defendants in a courtroom. At first I thought I would sit with them, but then reconsidered. Perhaps I could be more useful by maintaining a distance. We were seated at random, one hundred and twenty or so bishops. The gallery was small and crowded. The ordained women, the press, interested visitors, all were there. Others who could not crowd in peered through the doorway.

Bishop Allin began to speak. His Southern accent was strong, his bulldog face tense. We sympathized with his situation. "This is a most serious moment. . . . There is a crisis in the Church. We are here to reason together." He said that we were not to discuss whether women should be ordained priests, nor whether the Philadelphia ordinations were valid, but rather we were to concentrate on the narrower problem of order and discipline. First there would be an opportunity for general remarks. Then we would break into smaller groups for an informal exchange. Finally we would vote our common mind.

One by one bishops arose to state their views:

"We are a Catholic Church, governed by order and tradition. We cannot countenance the flouting of our most preciously held traditions."

"These bishops offended the Bishop of Pennsylvania. How would you feel if three of us came into your diocese without permission and tore up your pea patch?"

"What kind of deacons are these women who deliberately went against their bishops' express orders?"

"What would have happened, my brothers, if Luther had waited for an ecumenical council?"

"This is basically a matter of justice, when the canons of the Church must take second place. This very House, during the civil rights struggle, countenanced civil disobedience if conscience dictated it. Is the law of the Church more sacred than the law of the land?"

"Yes, but when we approved civil disobedience, it was only when all other means of redress had been exhausted."

"Well, I'm exhausted. Exhausted with this Church's continual compromise, continually putting itself above the welfare of the people and the justice of society."

I caught the eye of one of the ordained women. Her expression followed every word. Her life, at least her career, was at stake. It seemed bizarre that she was not allowed to speak for herself. But the privilege of the floor for the women had been voted down.

The question of ordaining women in the Episcopal Church was first raised in the House of Bishops in 1965, by the inimitable Jim Pike, Bishop of California. He was the apostle to those outside the Church, an enthusiast for the Word of God, which he tempered, some say altered, for the purpose of persuasion on points of justice and progressive thinking. At that time, Jim had ordained a woman to the order of deacon, claiming that this was basically the same as the order of deaconess, a long-standing status for women who wished to give their lives to the service of the Church but who were not called to the triple vows—poverty, chastity, and obedience—of the religious life of nuns. Deaconesses in those days wore a veil, received special training, and were made deaconesses in a special service conducted by a bishop. However, they never had been considered part of the threefold ordained ministry of bishop, priest, and deacon, which traditionally had been reserved for men. This threefold ministry had come down unchanged from the third century within the Catholic-style churches: Roman Catholic, Orthodox, and Anglican. The American Episcopal Church is part of the Anglican Communion.

I remember that House of Bishops meeting in 1965 well. It was in Great Falls, Montana. The Bishop of Montana presented the then Presiding Bishop with a young calf. The embarrassed bishop also had to don a headdress and be made an honorary chief of a local Indian tribe. This kind of stylized paternalism upset me. The discussions that week were monumentally boring. There was a heavily legalistic and institutional reaction to Bishop Pike's proposition. This was my first House of Bishops meeting, and I had looked forward to it. And there it was: a group of huffing, puffing, boring, institutionally protective executives, locked into preserving the Church at the expense of the world. Their eyes, I thought, were closed to reexamining the old ways. They seemed more concerned about the balance sheet of *The Episcopalian* (our Episcopal newspaper) than the national civil rights crisis.

My feelings then were self-righteous and idealistic, to be sure. I remember one night seriously considering resigning from what seemed to me to be a sorry mess. But I ran into Bob DeWitt on the way upstairs. "What on earth is the matter, Paul? You look awful!" he said.

"No, it's just this ghastly meeting," I replied. "Are they always like this? And why on earth is everyone so upset about this deaconess business? I don't necessarily agree with Jim Pike, but it doesn't seem to me that there is much difference between a deaconess and a woman deacon when you come right down to it."

"The only cure for how you're feeling is a stiff drink," Bob said. "I have a bottle of good bourbon and it's all yours."

Considering such an experience, I was not surprised nine years later in Chicago at how far removed I felt from the views of some of the brethren. And I knew that many of them had trouble with the likes of me, feeling that I played fast and loose with the stability of the Church and the sensitivities of their people in an overzealous concern for social issues like race, peace, or for that matter, feminism. I and bishops like me were rocking their boats by our public statements, our association with "extremist" groups, and the guilt we tended to lay on them when we spoke from the floor of the House.

After the opening remarks in plenary were over, we sat down in groups of ten or so in that depressing Chicago motel. The conversations took off rather quickly. All of us were trying to be restrained, trying to keep our feelings in check, trying to be objective and logical and respectful of one another's views.

Our group chairman began: "Perhaps we should define the limits of our assignment. We are not here to discuss the pros and cons of women's ordination, or even whether the Philadelphia ordinations were valid and irregular or totally invalid. Rather, we are here to discuss what we should do about the bishops who broke ranks and how we should treat the eleven women who were ordained in Philadelphia."

"But they weren't ordained, that is just the point."

"Slow down, Bill. We are not here to discuss that."

"Well, then, please don't refer to that fiasco as an ordination. And anyway, I do not see how we can discuss what to do with the bishops or the women unless we decide whether they were really ordained or not."

"I think they were ordained. All the elements were there—apostolically consecrated bishops, a valid liturgy, and the intent to ordain. What more does *your* theology require?"

"Let me say two things. First, an action outside the ordered life of the Church, an uncanonical action, does not hold water. Second, the 'matter' of the sacrament was not appropriate. To baptize you have to use water, to celebrate the Mass you need bread and wine, to ordain you need an adult male."

"You mean it doesn't 'take' unless the recipient is a male?"

"To put it crudely, that is exactly what I mean."

"Boy, let's unpack *that* one," someone muttered under his breath.

"I'm sorry, but I have to play the heavy as chairman. You are both out of order. We have to decide the issue. If we get into the substantive question we will be here for a week."

"Well, we need a week. We have never really discussed this question in the House from a theological point of view."

Another agreed. "This whole meeting was a mistake. We are all still too emotional about it to make sense."

"To get back to the subject. It seems to me there are three alternatives before the House," said a respected older bishop. "We can state that in our opinion the ordinations

were valid, if irregular, and proceed to recognize them and
to accept the women as priests in good standing in the
Church. Or we can state that the whole affair was completely
invalid, that the women are still deacons, and censor the
three bishops; or refer it back to a theological committee
to study and report to the next meeting of the House."

Once more in plenary session, the groups reported and
the Presiding Bishop appointed Bishop George Murray of
the Central Gulf Coast as chairman of an ad hoc committee
to make recommendations after lunch. Lunch consisted of
bad sandwiches and bad politics.

Bishop Murray's committee reported and some debate ensued, much of which was declared out of order by the chairman. The temptation to talk substance was constant. Then
the Bishop of Western New York moved for trial proceedings
against the erring bishops. Some of us, during a break, persuaded him to withdraw his motion. A motion to censure
was made. This was denied on the ground that it would prejudice a trial should a trial eventually be held. Finally, Murray
made a motion which was exceedingly ambiguous, contained
a negative in an unlikely place, and generally had the effect
of finding the ordination totally invalid—in a word, it had
not occurred. His motion took issue with the lawlessness
of the action. It further recommended a study of the issue,
and pastoral concern for the women ordinands.

I voted for the motion because it contained a rather mild
rebuke to the offending parties, with which I agreed, and it
promised time for more rational consideration of the real
issues by a study committee and concern for the ordained
women. However, before the roll-call vote had been completed, the wording was clarified to state that the Philadelphia
ordination was invalid, and I and several others changed our
votes to "abstain." A vote in favor of the motion carried
overwhelmingly; everyone wanted to go home. People were
even more angry than when they arrived in Chicago. When

we lifted our eyes after the final blessing, I found I had moved my seat to be beside the offending bishops, who were, after all, very close friends.

A strange event occurred on the way out of the meeting. As we walked into the hallway, we noticed a tight and eagerly listening crowd. A man was speaking. TV lights were on him. I recognized Charles Willie, the first black person ever elected vice president of the House of Deputies and therefore the next president of that House. Charles had been a moderate in the sixties. Now, as an observer at the meeting, he was extremely angry about the wrongs the women had just suffered at the hands of the bishops. He rehearsed the discrimination against blacks by the Church. All the resentment he must have harbored for years was flowing out in angry rhetoric. I thought to myself that I had never seen him like this. For a Harvard professor, he sounded less than academic. "And," he concluded, "I hereby resign my office as vice president of the House of Deputies and all other positions I hold in the national Church." Cheers came from the crowd. Microphones poked at his face for further comment. The historic special session of the House of Bishops was over.

That night on the plane back to New York I had a lot of thinking to do. Just before I left Chicago, I spent the afternoon with Bishop Corrigan, one of the offending bishops and a dear friend with whom I had worked and struggled over the years. Dan looks and talks like a farmer. He has a long face and dark, unbrushed hair. His expression is quizzical. He is one of the best-informed members of the House. My favorite story about Dan was when he and Eugene Carson Blake, the head of the National Council of Churches, attempted to integrate an amusement park outside Baltimore. A news photo showed Bishop Corrigan, in full bishop's clericals, sitting between two arresting officers, calmly reading the *New York Times* and waiting for a paddy wagon, clearly an enemy of the people. Dan tended to take a long view of things. I had never seen him ruffled. His rule of thumb was "Whenever you are faced with a difficult choice, go with the future, not the past."

I thought to myself on the plane that perhaps those errant friends of mine were right in ordaining the women. God knows, if it was these bishops against the former Bishop of Mississippi, the Bishop of the Central Gulf Coast, and the Bishop of Western New York, I would be on the side of the offending bishops. And yet they had made a mess. My own job would be harder: trying to avoid a trial in my diocese and also trying to keep the "irregular" women priests from having illegal services in New York. But this is the way progress comes, not smoothly through the system, but by disruption, reflection, and compromise. History moves in jerks, like an old steam engine pulling out of a station. Occasionally, I thought to myself, people fall down.

3

What Is to Be Done?

After the Chicago meeting, I was in for two years of tension and conflict. My job, as I saw it, was to hold the line until the General Convention in 1976 could pass legislation legitimizing the ordination of women to the priesthood. I wanted to prevent, if possible, charges being brought against the three irregularly ordained women in our diocese, and ecclesiastical trials. I had nightmares about newspaper headlines: "Inquisition on Morningside Heights" (our cathedral's location). "Liberal Bishop Accused of Sexism." I fantasized columns by Art Buchwald and Russell Baker, and cartoons in the *New Yorker*. People outside the Church would laugh. The one thing I cannot stand is the Church being an object of ridicule. Far better that we be an object of anger.

Soon after the Philadelphia ordinations, the ordained women celebrated the Eucharist at Riverside Church in New York City. This was within the geographical boundaries of the diocese, of course, but Riverside is not an Episcopal church. However, it was highly publicized and created a stir. On another occasion Carter Heyward officiated legally as a deacon at a service honoring the Archbishop of Canterbury. A priest, while receiving the Communion wine which she passed, deliberately scratched her hand and insulted her. A group called the Committee for an Apostolic Ministry was formed to oppose the ordination of women, and one of our clergy became its executive director. With such occurrences, the Diocese of New York might well have become the storm center of the controversy, and so be diverted from its overwhelming obligations to a desperate city.

These were the rough and tumble of events and personalities which would shape the future of this aspect of the Church's life. Beneath the surface, however, deeper streams were running. We Christians believe that the spirit of God can and does work through the confusions of history to bring about His will. We are never sure at the time what His will may be, but looking back to the Old Testament history of the people of Israel, the life of Jesus and His followers in the New Testament, and the life of the Church ever since, certain patterns do emerge. Great movements occur which later generations tend to agree are providential, even though, at the time they occurred, conscientious Christians or Jews battled to the death on either side.

A Christian view of history takes account of these mysterious tides and sees them as means by which people can learn more about the nature and purpose of God, can look deeper into their own selves, and can discover the strong bonds of life in their relationship with the heart and mystery of being we call God.

The clearest examples of this process occur in the Old Testament. The exodus of the Israelites across the Red Sea and through the desert to the Promised Land showed them that Jahweh was not only an all-powerful God of thunder and battle, but also a caring God. He would not prevent the suffering of His children, but He would lead them through suffering to their destinies with a guiding hand. To put it another way, this experience made the Jewish people believe that history had purpose and meaning, and that somehow the Almighty worked out this purpose through the weak and often ignorant actions of men and women.

Almost one thousand years later this same people was destroyed by the Babylonians, their sacred capital Jerusalem sacked, and their leaders sent into exile. A Jew could imagine no greater tragedy. And yet through the experience of exile they learned that Jahweh could also be worshiped outside the Holy Land: that the "mystery of being" was a unity rather than a plethora of tribal deities. Monotheism came into being. At about the same time the Jews discovered the possibility of individual salvation. A person could work out his individual destiny and was not entirely subject to the destiny of the whole community.

A more recent example of history occasioning theological insight occurred in the life of our own Church during World War I. Up to that time the Protestant aversion to prayers for the dead, brought about because of medieval abuse of this concept, was shared by the Anglican churches. During the war, however, the heartbreaking longing for a way to love a son, a husband, or a lover after death burst almost spontaneously into prayer for the departed. Thus out of the terror and tragedy of war came a renewed and graceful understanding of how human love could reach across death through the power of God's love.

The criteria by which I try to test the validity of change in doctrine are: Does this change give us a larger understanding of God and bring us closer to an understanding of Him as revealed in Scripture? Does this change liberate our spirit to become more fully human and nearer to the image of Christ? Does it reflect more clearly the image of God in which we are made? Therefore, does this change make us more compassionate, more just, more loving, and more free? If the change in thinking or practice accomplishes these goals, it is of God. However, if the change makes us have a smaller or more shallow understanding of God, or if it makes us more narrow of mind and spirit, the change is not of God. We bring to bear on these new understandings the ethical criteria gleaned from Scripture.

Jesus Himself said that we could not accept all He had to teach us but that the Holy Spirit would unfold what needed to be known. It is an understanding of this unfolding, this "revelation," that we seek in reading the Bible. The revelations found in the Bible are the criteria by which we judge the daily events and changes of life in the Church and in the world around us.

As a friend of mine who teaches at seminary put it, "The Bible can be thought of as a book of clues about the sort of things God does when He does things." Sometimes it is a small event that starts a theological revolution. A medieval monk, in the midst of a theological controversy, nailed his theses in anger upon the door of a church, and the enormous convulsion of the Protestant Reformation began in earnest. John Wesley heard the singing of the Mennonites during a storm at sea and experienced a spiritual enlightenment. From his subjective experience grew the Methodist Church. The ordaining of several women to the priesthood in a relatively small part of the Anglican Church, itself the smallest of the churches with Catholic structure and theology, may also become the event from which a major change in theology occurs. The very anger with which the occasion was received revealed the depth of its implications.

According to Catholic practice, the eucharistic liturgy is the most characteristic and essential action in which the Christian community participates. Its meaning is as deep and many-dimensioned as the event it commemorates. The Eucharist is a repetition of the Last Supper through which the communicants partake of Christ's death and resurrection. It is a holy moment in which the word of Scripture is heard and made our own. It is an acting out of the substance of Christian faith, and a common family meal of the gathered Christian community. The Eucharist is a reminder of the Christian's rebirth in baptism, and an actualization in the here and now of the role of "God-with-us" in Christ. It is an act of communion with Christ through which we share in His new life. The Eucharist celebrates God's creation and redemption, and anticipates his fulfillment of all things in the "heavenly banquet."

Although the whole congregation joins in the celebration of the eucharistic liturgy ("liturgy" means the "work of the people" of God), the one who presides, in Catholic tradition, must be an ordained priest or presbyter, who in this role "represents" Christ for the gathered people. This ordination can be performed only by a bishop in the succession coming down from the apostles (the "apostolic succession"), and it has to be carried out with the proper words, actions, and intent. The person to be ordained has had until now to be an adult male communicant. In recent times he has also had to be a deacon before he could become a priest.

Strangely enough, the concept of male priesthood has been so firmly established in tradition that no mention of its necessity occurs in Episcopal canon law.

The basic question about women priests is not whether women can be good administrators, counselors, pastors, or preachers, but whether or not they are proper subjects for ordination. Can one who is not a male symbolize Christ for His people and represent the people before God?

The resistance to the ordination of women is understandable. From earliest childhood a Christian hears God referred to as Father: "Our Father, who art in heaven . . ." Jesus referred to God as Abba, "Father." *Abba* is the Aramaic word by which children call their father, roughly the equivalent of "daddy." Furthermore, there is obviously no doubt that Jesus was a male. The Holy Spirit, the enigmatic third "person" of the Trinity, is referred to as "he" in liturgy, although a tradition of femininity surrounds the Holy Spirit in the Eastern Orthodox Church. (The name of the cathedral of Hagia Sophia in Istanbul means "holy wisdom," and "wisdom" is a feminine noun.)

On the other hand, St. Paul said that in Christ there is neither male nor female, nor has any respected theologian described God Himself as male. He is, by definition, beyond sexuality, or to put it another way, He embraces all reality in His being, including and transcending male and female. Since we are mortal men and women, however, we use analogies and word pictures as ways of describing God and His qualities. He is *like* a rock, *like* fire, *like* wind, *like* a fortress, *like* a father. We call Him Lord, Master, Creator. But when all is said and done, the average Christian or Jew images God as masculine and responds psychologically to God as a father.

The roots of the masculine quality of God go deep. The Jews were a patriarchal society and could not imagine the one and only ruler of the universe as being anything but male. Further, their first revelation of God came through the violence of their desert life. It was He who rode the thunder and shook the earth with volcanoes and earthquakes. It was He who sent them into battle, during which, in an occasional ecstatic experience, they felt one with Him. Small wonder, then, that this harsh, powerful, driving God should be thought of and felt as masculine.

For the skeptical modern mind, this projection of human qualities upon God raises problems of faith. Is God indeed a projection of the loving father, the *ideal* father, as Freud stated? And if this is true, does it mean that God is purely a figment of the human imagination with no objective reality? I believe that people do indeed project their feelings and ideas upon God, because an infinite, eternal being is so beyond the space and time limitations of the human mind that such projection is inevitable. But this does not invalidate the reality of God's existence. We know well that husbands tend to project the characteristics of their mothers upon their wives and often react to their wives as if to their mothers. However, this does not mean that their wives do not exist.

It means, rather, that they are distorting their understanding of their wives' persons by their own projections, and that they are responding to their wives in an emotionally inappropriate fashion. And so it is with our relationship to God. The analogies we use for Him are useful. They are a series of portraits each of which reveals one side of God's nature. However, if any single analogy assumes the ascendancy, the image of God is, by that much, distorted.

Take the example of God as Father. Say "father" to someone, and immediately the image of his own father comes into his mind. The image may be clothed with affection and he may feel a surge of love as he thinks of him. On the other hand, the image may be one of severity and judgment, or even worse, of rejection or desertion, in which case he feels a surge of fear and anger as he thinks of God. To different persons the word "father" means different things. If, then, each person uses the image "father" for God to the exclusion of others, his feeling and therefore his understanding of God will be distorted, and his relationship with God, called faith, will be affected.

Millions of people over thousands of years have thought of God as Father. Even though this thinking does not project an "old man with a beard" but just a psychic response to masculinity, it affects their image of God. It also affects their image of maleness as the ascendant gender. If God is male, not female, then men are intrinsically better than women. It follows, then, that until the emphasis on maleness in the image of God is redressed, the women of the world cannot be entirely liberated. For if God is thought of as simply and exclusively male, then the very cosmos itself seems sexist.

Within the Christian tradition, this problem is made more difficult by the doctrine of the Incarnation. This teaches that God made Himself personally present on earth by identifying Himself with a human person, Jesus of Nazareth. Thus people were allowed to meet and understand the infinite and eternal

God in the life of one human being. That human being, however, had to be either male or female; and Jesus of Nazareth was male.

We can deal with the problem of a masculine Christ if we understand the description of the Incarnation (the "enfleshing") given in the first chapter of the Gospel of John: "The Word became flesh and dwelt among us." What is said is that God became *flesh*, not that God became a *male;* and "flesh" here means simply "the human way of being," the bodily existence which belongs to all, male and female. If this is true, a woman can symbolically represent Christ in the Eucharist as well as a man. After all, the liturgy is not literal enactment but highly symbolic ritual. The Church believes in the priesthood of all believers, that all humanity shares in the priesthood of Christ. In the eucharistic liturgy, men and women both participate in the priestly acts of Jesus which are reenacted in the rite. There should be no bar, then, to women assuming the presiding role.

Worship is a subtle mixture of mind and feeling, of image and memory, of reasoning and intuition. As in the act of loving, the whole person is involved on every level of his or her being. The mind is involved as we contemplate the words. The memory is involved as we recall images and teachings and personal experiences. The feelings are involved when we experience affection, fear, guilt, joy, or sorrow. Belief, the content of faith, also stems from the total functioning of the person. The experience of worship feeds the understanding of belief. This has been true in my own life.

When, as a young man, I experienced the violence of battle in World War II, the blasphemy of war, I reached out to God for some way to deal with the bloodshed, the anguish, the shame, the fear, the sense that I was losing my mind. The image which came to me over and over again was the image of Christ on the cross. The crucifixion was a scene of violence, anguish, and fear. It touches the edges of insanity when Jesus's cry goes up, "My God, my God, why hast thou forsaken me?" But because God had turned that scene of horror into a symbol of hope, I could bear the experience of war, make it endurable. During my most terrible moments, I hung on to that great strong beam stretching across the universe, hung on to that great strong stake reaching to the sky. In war, I experienced in my own life some of the feelings which surrounded the crucifixion. Because of this, the cross has always remained at the heart of my personal faith.

Every human life on its own somehow relives the experience of the people of God through event, reflection, and revelation. When you grow old enough, you recite the creed and believe it as best you can intellectually. But it is only as you live out the implications of belief that you make it your own. You experience an event, reflect upon it, and find there a revelation of God. This is a never-ending process, this is the pilgrimage of faith.

Think of yourself in a church. The organ ceases, the service begins, the holy words are spoken. You hear a male voice. The holy words are always spoken in a low masculine voice. How often have you heard the words of Scripture enunciated by a man? How often by a woman? The thousands of times you have heard Scripture and prayer spoken in a male voice must have reinforced your feeling that God is male. God as Father and God as Son invoked by a male minister during worship creates in the unconscious, the intuitive, the emotive part of your belief an unmistakable male God. However, when women begin to read the Scripture, when they preside at the Eucharist, when they wear the symbolic robes of Christ, this unconscious perception will begin to be redressed and the femininity of God will begin to be felt.

I think people have always longed for the feminine in their worship. The cult of the Virgin in the Middle Ages, fostered by a celibate priesthood, was an example of this longing. I remember when I first sensed the power of the veneration of Mary and the feeling of joy that this presence was a reality in the life of the spirit. This realization came not through theological speculation but through meditation on the passage of Scripture describing the Annunciation, in which Mary accepts the vocation of being the mother of Christ.

I believe that in the human psyche, religious emotion and sexual feeling come from the same mysterious depths. The human life of love and the divine life of love are not separate, but part of the scope of God's love that sweeps through His creation. The love of a man for a woman, of a parent for a child, of a man for a man, a woman for a woman, the love of friendship or of passion all flow forth from a rich and powerful internal source of loving. And so does the love of a person for God. The Bible is full of examples of human love used to describe our love for God and God's love for us.

As I observed the vocation to priesthood of our women deacons, my intellectual belief that women should be ordained hardened into a firm commitment. Women have been allowed to be ordained as deacons since 1970. The order of deacon (servant) was instituted by the early apostles when they needed help with the pastoral ministry of feeding the hungry and ministering to the sick. It is an ordained order, but does not include the prerogatives of priesthood, the most important of which is celebrating the Eucharist.

As bishop of a diocese, I was delighted with our women deacons. Without exception the people they reached in their ministry responded to them with enthusiasm. Comments like: "I was against the idea of women ministers but when I got to know Carol as a person my whole attitude changed." "You will never know what Julia's ministry meant to me when I first heard I had cancer. I could relate to her as a woman in a way I could never relate to a man." "Barbara remains one of our finest teachers. Somehow her ordination gives her an added credibility."

The politics surrounding women's ordination continued

to build in the year following the Philadelphia service. Each side formed lobby groups looking forward to the General Convention in 1976, when the issue would be decided legally. The Diocese of New York was asked to help finance those advocating women's ordination. Strategy meetings were being held throughout the country.

I met with my clergy who objected to women's ordination and they were very decent about agreeing not to bring charges against the women who were illegally ordained. The price I paid for that promise was having to issue a strong letter condemning the Philadelphia ordination as irregular and making it clear that no priest in the diocese and no parish vestry would invite any of these women priests to officiate at their altars. This action kindled a sense of betrayal because the pro-women faction wanted me to ordain women priests before the General Convention and regularize the women ordained in Philadelphia. I refused to do either. I felt the Church needed more time to get used to the idea, and I resisted an illegal action. However, I felt like a cartoon published about me after I had refused to ordain the women deacons. The cartoon depicted me, on my bishop's throne, the ordinands before me, ready to be ordained, my hands tied behind my back.

In other dioceses events did not proceed so smoothly. Trials were held. Inhibitions (temporary suspensions from ministry) were leveled against offending clergy. Resolutions pro and con were passed by various ecclesiastical bodies. Women's ordination remained the main issue before the Church. We all waited for the convention, heartened by the fact that at their first meeting after Chicago, the House of Bishops voted in favor of the ordination of women to the priesthood by almost a two-thirds majority.

4

Is Honesty a Bar
to Ordination?

An even more explosive issue faced me toward the close of 1976: whether it was proper to ordain a homosexual person to the ministry. Four years before, one of our clergy, the Reverend Robert Weeks, had asked me to interview Ellen Barrett as a candidate for holy orders. He told me she was homosexual.

Bob Weeks was a rather eccentric fellow. He combined an Ivy League face, dress, and background with a strong and impulsive social conscience. His small urban parish was a scene of continual crisis, even chaos, as his good-humored, rather elderly vestry tried to keep up with him. First, the neighborhood programs got out of hand. Then he turned the church into a halfway house for prisoners. Father Bob Weeks was not cautious, not particularly ideological, never totally consistent, but always ready for an act of courageous loving. For him, like the Marines who trained him, strategy below the level of a division was thought to be muddleheaded. You simply charged ahead in a frontal attack oblivious to the losses. If you can imagine St. Francis as a Marine, it would give a fair hint of Bob's behavior pattern.

In 1972, Bob's cause was the gay movement. He himself was a straight arrow. He had a fine, attractive wife and several

40

children. His church, Holy Apostles in Manhattan, stands in the center of high-rise low-cost housing, like a small bird hiding in the forest. Its location on Ninth Avenue below Twenty-eighth Street is close enough to Greenwich Village and to Times Square to be easily available to the gay community. I do not know exactly how Bob became involved, but that year he asked my permission to rent his church on Sunday afternoons to the Church of the Beloved Disciple, a congregation of gay people. "Beloved Disciple" is a title given John in Christian tradition because he is referred to as "the one whom Jesus loved." The gay Christian community has adopted him as a sort of patron saint. The Church of the Beloved Disciple was born about the same time as the Metropolitan Community Church, another gay sect, but Beloved Disciple imitates a Catholic style of worship and now has elected its own bishop, while the Metropolitan Community Church is Protestant in tradition and practice.

I saw no reason to deny them the use of Holy Apostles so long as the vestry had no objections. Furthermore, Holy Apostles was often low on funds, and a few extra dollars a week would be a great help. I really did have premonitions of trouble, but being strong on civil rights, I felt they had a right to worship, whatever their predilections. I even met their pastor, at Bob's suggestion, and felt reassured when he said they were not interested in publicity.

I was a little gun-shy at that point in my life because a peace rally at our cathedral just the year before had gotten out of hand and it was reported in the media that pot was smoked and beer consumed in the nave. I did not need another crisis, especially one as touchy as gay rights. Hence my apprehension. Inevitably, before many months went by a New York newspaper published pictures with the headline "Gay Wedding at Holy Apostles Church." Most read it to mean that Father Weeks had performed the service. The fact that it was the gay church *using* the building did not come through clearly. Bob and I had a few searching conversations. I felt that the minister of the gay church had breached the spirit of our agreement about publicity. After a few more difficulties with their congregation, Bob and his vestry decided they should go.

I was not surprised when Bob called me to say that he was recommending an outspoken, homosexual woman to me for ordination to the diaconate. To say it came as no surprise is not to say I welcomed the news. I do try to avoid trouble, but when a question of conscience comes before me, I try to do the right thing without fearing the consequences too much. But I could just see that small dark cloud gathering on the horizon. "Look out, Paul," I said to myself, "this could be a wild one."

A candidate's approval for ordination has to be made jointly by the bishop and the diocesan Standing Committee. When I first became Bishop of New York, I discussed the issue of homosexual clergy with the committee. They approved a policy whereby if I knew "under the seal," or in confidence, that an applicant was homosexual and I felt him to be competent, stable, and of good character, I could recommend him to the Standing Committee in good conscience. However, we had never discussed the question of an applicant who had "come out of the closet."

Bob brought Ellen to see me in my office. I do not know what I expected, but I suppose unconsciously I had stereotyped the person I would meet: someone in masculine clothes, or dressed in a Greenwich Village kind of outfit. I expected a rather militant, even aggressive person who would put me immediately on the defensive. Despite my attempt to be without prejudice, I was shot through with it anticipating our meeting.

Bob, smiling as always, presented a slightly reserved Ellen, as if he were bringing a child to meet the principal of a new school. He said, "Paul, this is Ellen. I am sure you will like her," and then he excused himself and left the room. Ellen and I shook hands. I asked her to sit down on the sofa across from the wing chair where I usually sit when someone comes to see me. Ellen is tall, with dark brown hair conservatively styled. She, like many tall people, stoops a little as she walks. Her most arresting feature is her eyes, which appear honest, deep, and welcoming. After a minute or two you do not notice her steel-rimmed glasses. Her peaceful, warm expression gives you a sense of confidence and trust. In conversation, she seems rather soft, until the discussion finds its way into an area of faith or conviction. Then you strike rock.

Ellen did not seem a bit nervous, despite the importance of the occasion to her career. Nor was she intimidated by the surroundings. The office, located in a building on the Cathedral Close, has a huge stone fireplace with the bishop's coat of arms emblazoned (no other word will do) upon the stone above. Dark bookcases stretch thirty feet along the back wall, and large casement windows look out on a garden. This medieval atmosphere trembles from time to time when a truck passes, and reverberates to sirens and horns and the noises of the city. A young decorator and I worked hard to soften the ambience: bright curtains, Chagall prints over the fireplace below the coat of arms, a light tan carpet. There is a wing chair in front of the fireplace, and a yellow sofa and a coffee table on a warm Persian rug. The walls are white and the bookcases are open to display African art, ikons, chessmen, and other personal souvenirs. On a sunny day it is really a warm, bright room. But even so, a towering bishop in that atmosphere could be intimidating. Not, apparently, for Ellen. We started talking easily and soon I felt I knew her well.

"Well, Ellen, it's nice to see you after hearing so much about you from Bob."

"I wonder what he said," she laughed.

"He thinks a lot of you," I replied. "And of course he senses another crusade."

"Oh dear, I was afraid of that. I'm really no Joan of Arc, believe me."

"Nor am I the Grand Inquisitor!" I replied.

"No, seriously, I am only interested in ordination at this point. As you know, I have been involved in various gay organizations, but I'm really not a committee kind of person. And of course I did write an article or two about homosexuality. In those articles I made no secret of the fact that I am gay. But as soon as I seriously began to consider the ministry, I realized that my new sense of vocation and a more or less militant posture in the gay movement would not mix very well. So I have ceased to write articles. It is not that I am backing down, but rather that I want to put all my time and effort into becoming a deacon. I want to serve the Lord. I want to serve people and minister to them as best I can. I want to be a deacon."

"Well, Ellen, I would be kidding you if I said we don't have a problem."

I described our present policy, the makeup of the Standing Committee, and my own feeling that the diocese was not ready to deal with this question. We also discussed at length her background and how she made the decision to seek ordination. I pushed her hard to analyze her motivations.

In interviews like this I always try to see as deeply as I can into the person's mind and heart. How does someone know he or she has a "call" to the ministry, a "vocation"? In secular professions a person chooses a vocation on the basis of his or her skill, intellectual competence, family pressure or resistance to it, financial considerations, availability of job openings, and affinity to the field. Although many of these considerations apply to a vocation in the ministry, there is also a deep belief in a "call" from God. A passage from the Old Testament prophet Isaiah describes such a call and is often used in the ordination service:

In the year that King Uzziah died I saw the Lord sitting upon a throne, high and lifted up; and his train filled the temple. Above him stood the seraphim; each had six wings: with two he covered his face, and with two he covered his feet, and with two he flew. And one called to another and said:

> "Holy, holy, holy is the Lord of hosts;
> the whole earth is full of his glory."

And the foundations of the thresholds shook at the voice of him who called, and the house was filled with smoke. And I said: "Woe is me! For I am lost; for I am a man of unclean lips, and I dwell in the midst of a people of unclean lips; for my eyes have seen the King, the Lord of hosts!"

Then flew one of the seraphim to me, having in his hand a burning coal which he had taken with tongs from the altar. And he touched my mouth and said: "Behold, this has touched your lips; your guilt is taken away, and your sin forgiven." And I heard the voice of the Lord saying, "Whom shall I send, and who will go for us?" Then I said, "Here I am! Send me." And he said, "Go, and say to this people:

> 'Hear and hear, but do not understand;
> see and see, but do not perceive.' "

ISAIAH 6:1–9
(REVISED STANDARD VERSION)

Other passages in the Bible describe similar dramatic events, such as the story of St. Paul, who on the Damascus road was struck blind by a vision from Christ. But a decision to join the ministry also can be a long, slow process of coming to understand the will of God.

From one point of view, the dramatic conversion experience is the clearest indication of vocation. But an ecstatic religious experience might also indicate emotional instability. Even a long-standing sense of vocation can be problematical. I am always a little wary of anyone who does not go through some kind of intellectual or emotional rebellion during adolescence. As with one's human parents, from whom a breaking off and coming back is sometimes necessary to establish psychological independence and emotional maturity, so too with God the Father. On the other hand, sometimes young people who have grown up in a non-religious home seek religion as a means of rebellion.

Before an aspirant (the technical term for an applicant before he or she is accepted into any official category) reaches the diocesan bishop for an interview, he or she must be approved by the parish priest and vestry, and have been interviewed by a staff person for the ministries commission. In our diocese this was Bishop Wright, one of our suffragan bishops. The aspirant then attends a screening weekend with selected clergy and laity of different backgrounds and skills. If the screening process is positive, he or she has a medical and psychological examination. All aspirants must have academic credentials and submit an autobiographical statement.

The diocesan bishop, with all this background, is now ready to interview the aspirant. Even so, it is hard to sift through the mixture of spiritual, emotional, intellectual, and practical considerations that go into such a decision. A generation ago, if a young man was competent academically and had nothing obviously wrong with him, he was approved, because the Church was in urgent need of clergy. Now, because we have caught up with the shortage of men caused by World War II and the suburban explosion of the Church in the 1950s, and because inflation has diminished the number of full-time positions open in the Church, we have more clergy than we can use. In New York we have at least fifty applicants for parish jobs each year, and can place only three or four of them. Thus, our present screening process is much more selective.

A further complication is that a new category of priest has recently emerged. Called non-stipendiary priests, they can earn their living in the secular world and remain in good standing by carrying out a ministry in their free time.

When someone comes to me for an interview I try to use my intuition, as well as my reason, to sense if there is commitment and stability, toughness and dedication. Ellen's responses seemed authentic. Her thinking was clear. She seemed to have an unusual amount of self-understanding, and no illusions about the world or the Church. The only thing I was not sure of was whether she had lived long enough with her vocation to have it take root and to be able to withstand whatever pressures might come in her ministry. I also, frankly, had my own doubts about the wisdom of ordaining someone who was so open about her sexuality. I was almost certain the Standing Committee would not approve her.

In an hour's conversation, Ellen told me about her childhood in the South, her first exposure to the Church, and her reasons for disclosing her homosexuality. During the interview I was racing around in another corner of my mind to find what I might say to this rather extraordinary young woman when the interview was over. I said, "I think I have come to know you a bit today, and I am impressed with what I have found. You have the qualifications, as far as I can determine, to be a good deacon or priest, when that becomes possible. However, I do not think the Standing Committee will pass you, and to be honest, I am not sure they should, at this point. I myself don't know what I think about your open homosexuality, but I do know that most of the diocese would be surprised if not shocked by it. Also, I think you need to live with your vocation for a while. In any case, I will discuss this with the Standing Committee as an issue, without using your name."

"I understand," she replied. "I won't pretend that it does not hurt. I intend to go to seminary anyway, since I want to teach in the field of religion or medieval history."

"I am glad I have gotten to know you," I said. "I feel I

can be straightforward with you, and I am relieved because we probably have a ways to go on this one before we are through."

"Goodbye. Thank you."

"God bless you, Ellen. I think He will help us find the best way."

After she left I asked not to be disturbed and went back to the wing chair to think and pray. I began to see the issue squarely. Here was someone well qualified whom I would pass without hesitation, if she had not come out publicly as a gay person. Is such candor and honesty and courage a bar to ordination? Or putting it another way, is not such exhibitionism and "flaunting" of one's sexuality cause for scandal in an ordinand? It depended how you looked at it, and also on the motivation for the disclosure. But such a decision also involved the impact on the Church. This was the beginning of long hours of self-questioning in the months ahead.

I introduced the issue at the next meeting of the Standing Committee. As I had anticipated, they decided in principle that at that time they could not consider an openly declared homosexual for ordination. Some of their views were depressingly familiar: "I have many good friends who are homosexual. I even have had some to dinner. But I would not want one for a parish priest." "A priest is supposed to be a Christian model. How can a homosexual person be a model?" "I surely would not want my children exposed to such a priest." "Whether it's right or wrong, the diocese couldn't stand it. It would rip the churches apart. In fact, I tell you right now, if this committee passes such a person for ordination, I am going to resign publicly and say why in no uncertain terms."

Others were more moderate. "I know many very good parish priests who I am sure are homosexual. Everybody who isn't completely naïve knows it. And yet nothing is said and they have effective ministries." "That's just the point. People shouldn't talk about their sex lives. It isn't dignified, especially for clergy. That's why bathrooms have doors!"

As I remember it, no formal vote was taken. The implicit consensus was that the committee would not approve a declared homosexual person for the priesthood.

The trouble with a job like mine is that you really can't win! Although a bishop does not have to be elected more than once, the position is political in that to accomplish anything, to assume any kind of leadership, you have to have people behind you. My sigh of relief because the Standing Committee's decision meant that I would not have to confront the angry opposition was short-lived. Soon after I told Ellen that she could not be accepted as a candidate at this time, her rector telephoned me.

"Bishop, Ellen told me the news."

"Yes, Bob."

"She is very disappointed."

"I know that, Bob."

"Just wait until the gay community hears about this. There is going to be an enormous reaction. I hate to say it, Bishop, but despite our friendship I may have to organize a picket line in front of your office." (Incidentally, Ellen had no part in such plans.)

I was beginning to feel like a reactionary. "Wait a minute, Bob. We are just beginning even to talk about this. You have to let people have a little time."

"Bishop, I never thought I would hear you, of all people, sounding like those white Southerners, sounding like a . . . a . . . a . . . 'gradualist!' " That was the worst epithet you could earn in the sixties.

"Bob, that really is not fair." I was starting to whine and be defensive.

"Fair! Do you think it's fair to be a gay in America? They are the most persecuted minority around. Fair, indeed!" he snorted.

"Come on, Bob. Enough of the rhetoric. The simple fact

is that the Standing Committee won't approve a homosexual, and I have to be honest and say I think they are right. The backlash would be incredible."

"Bishop Moore," he said (Bob always became more and more formal the angrier he was), "are you going to keep someone from being a deacon just because she is honest?"

He really had me on that one. That was the question that kept bothering me for the next three years; that was the question that I knew I would someday have to confront. "Are you going to keep someone from being a priest just because she is honest?"

"Bob, that's the way it is. Even if you could convince me, the Standing Committee will not budge. And, as I told you, I think they are right."

"This isn't the last of all this, I assure you," he said ominously, and hung up.

Sexual feelings for a person of the same sex have been part of the human experience for thousands of years. No one knows why it occurs or why it appears more prevalent at particular times in history. Were there more homosexual persons in ancient Greece than in Israel, or was it that those in Greece could express these feelings without fear? Is the taboo against homosexuality in some cultures a sign of cultural strength or weakness? Did the taboo occur because the society needed children to tend the farm, or was it an intuitive aversion to something "unnatural"?

The Judeo-Christian religion and the culture surrounding it have been traditionally against homosexuality. Indeed, our traditional morality has been against any sexual activity outside marriage. In reality, illicit sexual desire between a man and a woman has been winked at. Literature is full of love poems to unattainable women. Dante sang of Beatrice, Lancelot longed for Guinevere. This love, though forbidden, has been allowed public expression. Even sexual activity outside of marriage, although officially immoral, is condoned. Young men "sow wild oats," and in fact, are admired for their lustiness. But the slightest indication of sexual love between persons of the same sex is looked upon with horror.

We had no name for it when I was growing up, but machismo was the goal for an American boy in the 1920s. You had to play baseball or football whether you liked it or not. The humiliation of not being a good player was extremely painful. I can still remember dropping a forward pass in a school football game. I remember sitting on the sidelines, terrified that someone might think I was a "sissy" because of my lack of athletic competence. The fact that I was a passable tennis player, golfer, rider, and sailor was no comfort. These were not "contact" sports.

How many thousands of American boys underwent this torture? It never occurred to me until recently that this fear was a projection of homophobia by society. Not having a talent for sports has nothing to do with homosexuality whatsoever, and yet the fear of homosexuality lay behind the fear of not having a full "masculine" identity.

This shame at not being an athlete intensified when I attended a boarding school where athletic prowess was the way to popularity and success. Only grudgingly were other abilities like scholarship acknowledged. Furthermore, any hint of homosexuality was reprehensible. I remember four younger boys who were discovered in a compromising situation by one of the school's masters. Rumors flew around the school that they were about to be expelled. We sensed an abhorrence on the part of the authorities, and a difference in the way this was discussed from other rule breaking, such as smoking.

All kinds of myths about sex circulated at school. Some said masturbation would lead to insanity. Others recommended it as a way of growing! A great deal of excitement surrounded sex. It was forbidden fruit, so to speak, because

our parents never mentioned it. However, as small boys we
had no self-consciousness regarding homosexuality. Until homophobia was projected upon us from the adult community,
it did not exist in our minds. Gradually, as we grew up, we
absorbed these prejudices from the surrounding culture.

At first the influence was indirect and had to do with deep
anxiety about measuring up to the image of the typical athletic
American boy. Then came flashes of adult panic when some
incident arose and was discussed behind closed doors. Jokes
about "fairies" were a part of the adolescent sophistication,
and of course these jokes were aimed at whoever was suspi-
ciously unmarried in the adult community or seemed effemi-
nate to the students. The reality of homosexuality remained
a taboo mystery clouded in shame and fear.

I am sure these rambling memories are not unusual. But
I am convinced that the early anxieties surrounding sexual
identity are behind the unreasoning rage occasioned by the
ordination to the priesthood of a woman homosexual in 1976.

How similar sexual myths are to racial myths which arise
to create an atmosphere of hatred and contempt. "Niggers
are lazy." "Fairies can't play football." "Niggers are dirty."
"Bachelors are queers." "Integrated schools lead to inter-
marriage." "Would you want your daughter to marry a
Negro?" "Homosexuals shouldn't teach school because
teachers are role models." "Would you want your daughter
to grow up a lesbian?" (Russell Baker in his *New York Times*
column, during the Anita Bryant controversy, stated that despite the fact that all his teachers in grade school were spin-
sters, he never wanted to grow up to be a spinster!)

In the past, racial prejudice found its ultimate expression
in lynchings and burnings, which, in a perverse way, substantiated our prejudice: mustn't the offense have been very great
to warrant lynching? Homosexuals too were lynched and even
burned to death in former times. In the sixties there was a
superstition that Negros wanted to rape white women, which

was co-mingled with a sexual fear about black sexual prowess. This both thrilled and terrified the white community. Even today homosexuals are suspected of child molesting, despite the fact that heterosexual molestation is much more commonly reported.

The same dangerous mythology that has kept black people in a position of degradation in this country and led to the extermination of the Jews in Nazi Germany surrounds our society's treatment of homosexuality. Just as white Southerners have used the Bible to justify their racial prejudice, so do we use the Bible to justify our discrimination against homosexual persons. This mythology is a dangerous mix of sex, violence, and religion.

Nor were we given any objective information by which to combat all this. We were taught in eighth-grade biology about the mechanics of sex. I suppose even that was advanced for a church school in 1933. We were told not to worry about masturbation, that "everybody did it." But beyond that nothing was said about sex. Nothing about the emotions of sexuality, of what went on between a man and a woman. Nothing about marriage or about sexual development. And of course, nothing was said about homosexuality. We were left to our own devices in seeking knowledge about sex and establishing our own sexual attitudes, a risky business, given the sexual misinformation which came our way. It is hard to remember what life was like in a pre-Freudian culture.

Even today, despite our modern advances in the understanding of human psychology, most Americans have not allowed an understanding of homosexuality to inform their thinking. The enlightened propaganda of gay activism when advanced on television or in newspapers and magazines still falls on deaf ears. People are too threatened even to listen or to discuss the issue calmly.

Although most church members had never dealt with this matter, a few farsighted church leaders had been exploring the moral implications and psychology of homosexuality for some time. In the late 1940s, the British parliament appointed a commission made up of jurists, doctors, and churchmen to examine the English laws concerning homosexuality. The so-called Wolfenden Report was the result of their deliberations. It recommended that sexual relations between consenting adults no longer be considered a crime. This would include homosexual relations. The Wolfenden Report is a landmark, because for the first time an official government body dared to consider homosexuality rationally. The purpose of law is not to enforce morality but to protect the community. The commission made the very sensible observation that what two persons do in private does not endanger the rest of the community. It is significant that some churchmen, including Church of England bishops, signed the report.

In our own Church, a committee of the House of Bishops called the Pastoral Committee began considering the problem of homosexuality among the clergy in the early 1960s. The matter was discussed by the whole House behind closed doors. I was not a bishop then and do not know the gist of the discussions. However, when I became a bishop I was appointed to the Pastoral Committee and homosexuality was the subject which came up most frequently. We had several all-day sessions with psychiatrists, and each bishop was advised by the committee to have a consulting psychiatrist assist him. One of the most active psychiatrists in the field was Dr. Margaretta Bowers, whose book *Conflicts Among the Clergy* contains case histories of homosexual clergy. What a tragic compendium it is.

In my own life there was one such priest to whom I was close over a period of thirty years.

5

The Story of John

I first knew John when he was a young priest in a suburban parish. He was popular as a young unmarried clergyman and had a certain polish from his year of studies in England. Among a sophisticated group of people his Anglophile ways, his family silver and old ship prints were admired. John bought his shirts at Brooks Brothers and his tweeds in England. He smoked a pipe and made something of a fuss about having the right tobacco. In his library some rare editions of the Book of Common Prayer stood next to the works of E. F. Benson, A. E. Housman, and romantic stories of young Englishmen at Eton and in the First World War.

John was a little over six feet tall and wore his hair short, according to the style in those days. He was something of an athlete and jogged earnestly every afternoon long before jogging was fashionable. But the most attractive part of his personality was his sense of humor. He was one of the finest storytellers I have ever heard. There were many evenings when he would entertain his young friends with stories as we sat in front of his fire and inhaled the smell of good tobacco, old leather, and burning wood. In the firelight he told us about the heroes of the Church. We saw Father Breboeuf and his comrades stand fast in the faith as they were burned at the stake by the Indians. We thrilled at Francis's rebellion against his rich father in the square at Assisi, his tearing off his fine raiment in public and giving himself to his Lord, to follow Jesus in poverty. We spent many hours, or so it seemed, with Father Wainwright, Father Dolling, and Father Wilson in creaky old rectories in the London slums at the turn of the century. Charwomen came to the door looking for "Father," their little children dying. Cabbies would pick Father up in the middle of the night to take him on some errand of mercy. Father stood strong for the rights of the poor and brought them the strength and love of Jesus in their suffering. The stories contained smiles and chuckles at the eccentric ways of the priests and the clumsy kindness of the poor. And then there were stories of the British navy, of admirals and sailors, of lords and ladies, of so-and-so who was a "terrific snob." Once in a while he shared harmless parish gossip with us. This made us feel "grown up" as we detected feet of clay among the adults of the community.

John was an incurable romantic. He was in love with England, and with the saints. He loved the Church in all its eccentricity. Sometimes the liturgy of the tweeds and pipes and old silver became indistinguishable from the liturgy of the Anglo-Catholic movement. John was a High Churchman. He would sneak us away from school on a snowy afternoon to some outlandishly High Church parish where we vested and walked in procession with priests in their birettas behind banners of the Virgin Mary, and our young nostrils twitched with the unaccustomed fumes of incense. But at the solemn moment of benediction a sense of reverent awe and mysticism we had never known at morning prayer in the parish church touched our souls and we sensed that beneath the color and strangeness was a Presence before which we knelt in wonder.

One day an old monk from England visited us and I made my first confession to him. That was my moment of conversion. John, with great delicacy, channeled my adolescent emotions and brought me to the Eucharist where this new and awesome dimension of my life found its expression. Often thereafter I·served at an early Mass, as we liked to call it, and in the cold church the words "This is My body, this is My blood" spoke directly to me.

John loved his kids, loved the people of the parish, loved the Church and, as I look back, was beginning to find his own way into a more serious priesthood. And he laughed a lot. Laughed at himself and laughed at the ironies of a life where ordinary and sinful people were touched from time to time by the glory of the Kingdom.

John moved to another parish, but I saw him now and again. He never presumed to be my spiritual adviser, but with a wise reticence guided me to other older and holier priests. He was more like an older brother in my life, or perhaps a young father who seemed to understand me far better than my own.

The war came. His beloved English navy was once more on the high seas, with the flag flying and the chaplains on board. But there was nothing romantic about the newspaper headlines. This was not Lord Nelson and his gallant crew. This was a tanker in the cold North Sea going down with all hands. I sensed now, when we talked, a realism that had not been in our conversation before. John was beginning to realize that he might, before long, have to be a participant in the life he had only read about in the past.

He enlisted as a chaplain in the Army, and when America entered the war he went overseas with his unit—not to England, but to Southeast Asia. I did not hear from him much, and before long I was in the Marine Corps and communication became even more difficult. I did hear through a mutual friend that something bad had happened to him and that he was no longer in the Army.

When the war was over I returned to New York and looked him up. He was living with his aunt in Rockland County. I went out to see him. As he opened the door of a little house in an old part of the town, I saw an older man in the shadows, slightly stooped. His manner was nervous, and his discomfort and embarrassment that we should meet in such surroundings almost overcame his gentlemanly charm. He asked if we could go for a drive. We got into the car and drove aimlessly around. A car is an easy place to talk. You don't have to look at each other. The embarrassment of silence is disguised by absorption in the passing scene.

First we talked superficially about mutual friends and where we had been in the war. Finally he began to tell me what had happened to him. He had been with his unit in the jungle for over a year. There was little action, no amenities, few if any congenial friends. John started to drink in earnest. He apparently had had something of a problem with this earlier. One night when he was drunk he took a walk with a soldier on the beach. As they sat together on that lonely shore, John reached out to him in love. The boy became frightened, and reported the incident. A court-martial followed. John was dishonorably discharged and immediately deposed from the priesthood. Before long he found himself in Rockland County, living with his aunt with no vocation, no job, no money, and the most enormous shame I have ever known anyone to carry.

I guess I had known, in fact I am sure I had known in the old days, that John was homosexual. He had no women friends to speak of. Photographs of boys he had befriended were displayed around his room. However, he never to my knowledge made an advance to any of us. Somehow this side of his nature was not offensive. I had had many teachers at school who were bachelors. They always had more time for us than the married men had and seemed a little more concerned for us. In any case, I was not surprised at what John told me. But I was stunned and hurt and angry for him. It simply did not make sense, that a momentary gesture of affection, no matter how misguided, could destroy a man's life. I had learned a lot in the war, but I was not prepared to deal with this. Now the roles were reversed; my former priest and mentor was dependent upon me. All I could do that day was to say how sorry I was. We had a cup of coffee at a diner, the first of so many, and I dropped him off at the miserable little house in the wrong part of town. As he waved goodbye, dressed in his tweed jacket and button-down shirt, he gave me his old smile. I thought how he might have told this story about such a person as himself as we sat by his fire in the safety of those early days.

Another friend of his and mine helped him get a job in a bookstore. Before long, however, he began to be late to work and was fired. He was drinking. The first of many attempts to dry out followed. Then another job in another bookstore. Again unexplained absences. One night I was studying for an examination at seminary. It was about midnight when the phone rang. "Paul, it's John." His voice was slurred. "Can you get me something to eat? I am without funds."

"Where are you? I have an exam tomorrow."

"I'm at the Men's Hotel just north of Times Square. What will happen to me? I don't have any money and I haven't had anything to eat for a day."

"Okay, John. I'll come."

I went up there, picking up a sandwich and a large container of coffee on the way. I went into a lobby that looked like a police station. Cement floor, stucco walls, one or two benches, a desk. I asked for John. The man behind the desk gave me a room number and looked at me with some suspicion, I guess because I was dressed in a suit that was neat. The elevator and the corridor smelled of disinfectant. I knocked on the door. A young man in blue jeans let me in. John was on the bed with a two-day growth of beard, his Brooks Brothers shirt dirty, his tweed jacket thrown over his feet. Two youths sat on straight chairs. I sat in the easy chair in the corner. The boy who had let me in looked me over.

"I'm a friend of John's," I said.

"Oh, yeah. Okay."

I looked over at John. "How are you?"

"Awful. I can't speak. I'll try to eat this later. These are some friends of mine."

The boy who had let me in came over and sat on the arm of my chair. There was nowhere else to sit, so there was not much I could do about it. "Yeah," he said. "We're hustlers. John is a good friend of ours. Where do you live?"

"My family and I live down on Twenty-first Street."

"My God, he's straight." The boy jumped up and sat on the floor. They were friendly kids, seventeen to twenty years old. Seeing them sitting around John's room was a macabre reenactment of those days around the fireplace in his study, when a different group of boys listened to his stories. But somehow, even now, John had shown them he cared about them. Even now, in a strange way he was acting out his priesthood.

Over the next twenty years I stayed in touch with John. Time after time he would begin a new job, have a few good months, then the drinking would begin again. I sent him off to the country to stay with a priest in Vermont. He returned and in a little while began the drinking again. Then he tried a two-month visit at a monastery. Same result. As the bouts grew worse he tried private hospitals and psychiatric sessions. No change. Finally the expense of these treatments became inordinate and he wound up at Bellevue. Next time in, he was transferred to a state hospital on Long Island.

Even at this hospital, when he was not in the fatigues that patients wore for work, he dressed in his Brooks Brothers outfits with a regimental tie. He cultivated gentlemanly relationships with the Episcopalians on the staff, and chatted about Harvard with the one doctor who had a Harvard undergraduate degree. And of course he continued to make friends with other patients, especially young men who were drawn to him as to a father. From time to time he would refer one of these young people to me, and I would try to be helpful and exchange professional views with John about the young man's progress. I remember one visit I made on a summer's day. I found John sitting on the grass, surrounded by a few odd-looking young men with slightly deranged expressions, telling them stories about the Jesuits and the Iroquois and the London priests at the turn of the century.

Whenever possible, he came over to our church in Jersey City, where he was loved and admired by the extreme variety of people who came and went in our inner-city rectory. John was great with the "porch set," our euphemism for the alcoholic men who came to the rectory for a meal. He was good with the kids, of course, and carried the Sunday dinner conversations along on a level appropriate for his audience, which might have been an old college friend of mine, or my elderly mother, or a boy just out of prison, or the bishop's Victorian wife.

When dinner was over and he had had a last pipe in the living room, he would say goodbye and wander down the walk onto the lonely street, bound for his furnished room in Hoboken, or for Times Square.

One story he told about himself still remains clear in my memory. He had made a special friend of a young man he had met in Times Square. He told me that the young man never solicited him, even when John had some money. They would meet, have a cup of coffee, then take the subway to Coney Island, or to the Cloisters, where John told him stories about St. Francis and St. Louis, and why the Virgin Mary was held in affection by the medieval clergy. They would often picnic together in Central Park after a trip to the Morgan Library to see the Gutenberg Bible. When the chill of evening came into the air they would get on a bus for the long ride home, and the young man would fall asleep with his head on John's shoulder. A little love there in that darkened bus, a moment of warmth, a time for dreaming.

John never gave up. His periods outside the hospital
lengthened until he won a discharge. Meanwhile I had been
working to reverse his dishonorable discharge from the Army
and, if possible, gain his reinstatement as a priest. Some
twenty-five years after that tragic night on the beach in the
South Pacific where he had reached out in love to a soldier,
his dishonorable discharge was removed and he was reinstated as a priest.

A few good years followed in which he became a part-
time chaplain at some city hospitals. When I was elected a
bishop I asked John to be one of the two clergy to present
me. I remember his face in the great crowd at the Washington
Cathedral, and I thought of the Jesuit martyrs and the priests
of the London docks. His eyes were looking up, and he too,
I'm sure, was remembering a fireplace and a group of kids
long, long ago.

A few months later he had a relapse and went back to
the state hospital. One morning as he was getting ready to
go home, prepared as never before to carry on a priesthood
informed by all that pain and love, he collapsed and died.
We buried him with a solemn requiem and filled the church
with the incense smoke he loved so well.

I have a chest of polished wood which belonged to him.
Inside are a chalice, a paten, and two cruets of old English
silver. John had given it to me when he was deposed. I had
it refurbished and presented it to him the day he was reinstated. He left it to me in his will. When I look at these
vessels I hear the words of Christ, which John and I had
said so often, "Do this in remembrance of Me."

I wonder what his priesthood would have been had his
case been handled with more understanding. For was it not
through John that I first was converted to the Christian faith
which has filled my life? Through the persistence of his priesthood and through the chaos of his later years I learned how
deep a vocation can reach and how the grace of priesthood

can burst forth in glory in unlikely times and places.

Since I have been a bishop I have had to deal with similar difficulties in the lives of priests. Thank God, all of them have been able to continue their ministry. Most had to leave the parish where they worked. All received therapy so that they could better understand the forces which were driving them. One later married and raised a family. And, of course, I have known of heterosexual indiscretions, but they don't arouse the panic surrounding homosexual incidents, and therefore can be dealt with more reasonably. I remember one homosexual incident when I was called up by the police in the middle of the night and told that if I did not get a priest out of town in twenty-four hours he would be locked up.

In recent years the Church has become more informed. Bishops have continued to educate themselves, but the education has often been only skin deep. I remember a discussion I had with a dozen bishops and a psychiatrist. After convincing evidence was given about the emergence of homosexuality in a person without his choosing it, some bishops still insisted a person could change if only he wanted to enough. Others said they would never ordain a homosexual person, period. And others, who themselves were more open-minded, could not deal with the strong anti-homosexual feelings of their people. It was far easier for all of us, whatever our views, simply not to talk about these things. We feared, with justification, the depth of feeling that could be released when the issue was confronted.

This was the prevailing attitude of the Church when Ellen came to my office in 1972 and was turned down in her first attempt to be ordained.

After being turned down here, Ellen went to see Bishop DeWitt in Philadelphia, hoping that he might accept her as a candidate. Bob DeWitt took her in, encouraged her, but, like me, could not bring her past his Standing Committee.

If she could not be accepted in New York or Philadelphia, clearly all doors were closed. Ellen, however, still wanted a theological education. She enrolled at General Theological Seminary in New York and built a fine academic record there. I saw her from time to time. Our relationship was a little distant, but cordial.

I think it was early in 1975 when Ellen came to see me again. She said she still wanted to be ordained and felt there was no harm in asking if we would reconsider. Ellen's record at seminary was splendid. The faculty thought highly of her academically and spiritually. It seemed to me that her sense of vocation had been proven more deep than most, and that her association with the gay movement was secondary to her desire to be ordained. She had made no speeches, written no articles for the movement in the last three years. It seemed unjust that she should be forever barred from ordination. I decided it was time to allow her to go through our screening system and see whether the Standing Committee would take another look at the situation. Two years had passed. Many articles on the subject had appeared in the media. Gay rights bills had been debated. Our own diocesan convention had passed a resolution backing the local effort for gay rights in New York. The general atmosphere was slowly changing.

Ellen passed the screening conference, and I recommended her to the Standing Committee. Because of its clarity and inclusiveness, I think it useful to include the Standing Committee's later statement concerning their action in its entirety.

February 14, 1977

To Whom It May Concern

Re: The Ordination of The Rev. Ellen Marie Barrett

A good deal of correspondence and publicity has been addressed to the ordination of Ellen Marie Barrett. We are writing to state our conception of the decisions made by this committee in the past in connection with that ordination. Our purpose is neither to justify nor to apologize, but rather to explain the actions taken in hopes that support or criticism of the Standing Committee and bishops involved with the ordination will be addressed to the issues they considered, and not to other issues. These issues may be faced, and may have been faced, by other Standing Committees, which may benefit by a statement of our experience.

Members of the Standing Committee of our diocese are elected by the diocesan convention, in which parishes are represented proportionate to their membership. The decisions in question were made over a period of several years. Only three members of the current committee were members when the first decision was presented for a vote. Twelve elected members of the committee have been involved in one or more of the four decisions made. All votes on the subjects discussed herein were unanimous except the most recent, in which one dissenting vote was cast. Of the current committee, two members are opposed in principle to the action taken.

There are many other people involved in every ordination in the Diocese. A proposed rector and vestry, the Ministries Commission, a screening conference composed of clergy and laity, a seminary faculty, a psychiatrist and a bishop must approve a candidate before ordination can take place. Thus, many devoted churchmen have been involved in this case with decisions similar to ours; no one church authority bears sole responsibility. Nevertheless, a major portion of the responsibility belongs to the Standing Committee.

The issue faced by the committee on four separate occasions can be simply stated as follows:

Should a person who is in all respects otherwise qualified be denied ordination to the priesthood of our church because that person openly acknowledges homosexual orientation?

The committee answered this question in the negative on four occasions, three times by unanimous vote.

Some will find it difficult to conceive that a person openly acknowledging homosexual orientation can be otherwise in all respects qualified for ordination to the priesthood. Others will conclude, perhaps on the basis of extraordinary national publicity, that Ellen Marie Barrett is not in fact otherwise qualified. On the basis of information available at the time votes were taken, the committee and all other groups in the process decided that she was qualified, and thus the committee faced squarely the narrowed issue stated above.

No decision on the part of the committee and our bishops to approve the ordination of any person has ever been a political act in support of any liberation movement. Beyond this, the issue as framed by the committee does not allow for an interpretation that the committee approved the ordination out of concern for an oppressed minority group. No ordination decision can be generalized without regard to the vocation of the individual ordained. Thus, it was not the purpose of any member who voted in favor of the candidacy and ordination either to approve or disapprove, or to encourage or discourage, any form of sexual conduct for members of our church generally.

The committee has never taken the position that all forms of sexual behavior are irrelevant in considering the qualifications of a candidate. In the case of Miss Barrett, the committee did not decide that licentious, promiscuous or notorious sexual behavior are acceptable in a person seeking ordination. A majority of the committee believes that Miss Barrett is not such a person.

In the case of Miss Barrett, the committee did not decide that one who advocates homosexual behavior by others, or influences children to become homosexuals, should be ordained. A majority of the committee believes that Miss Barrett is not such a person.

The committee was not presented with these questions, regardless of recent publicity in the national press causing others to frame the issue in such terms. Allegations in current press coverage that were presented to the committee at the time were explained by Miss Barrett to the satisfaction of the committee at the time. If the committee had believed all current allegations, further inquiry might have been required.

Some who are critical believe that all of these questions are inherent in the word "homosexual," whether or not facts confirming perverse sexual behavior are alleged. The members of the committees who voted to approve her candidacy and ordination were not encumbered by such inherent images. The committee was no more aware of any specific sexual practices of this candidate than of those of many other candidates, heterosexual or covert homosexual.

At the same time, the committee did not require a commitment to abstinence as a condition to ordination. Some correspondence and discussion has drawn a distinction between "orientation" and "practice." The committee did not draw such a distinction.

Much of the responsible criticism comes from theologians and people with training in psychology, with whom other theologians and psychologists disagree. Apparently, many people have clearer views on this subject than any member of this committee or any bishop involved in the actual decisions has ever had. For some, the Bible produces this clarity of view, and for others a natural law, or psychological axiom grants undeniable guidance. Many believe that ordination should have been denied simply because of projected controversy.

Suffice it to say that none of these principles was determinative to the committee that made the decisions. The dialogue continues, within the committee and without. If the issue stated above is as pervasive as some think it is, the committee position may change as a result of subsequent elections. In this uncertain and developing context, we can only look for guidance to the Holy Spirit, trusting that any mistakes made by any of us will be corrected.

In the meantime, the committee will continue to approve only individuals determined to be highly qualified by the diocesan selection process, considering, as always, vocation to the priesthood and commitment to the Body of Christ to be the dominant prerequisites.

Respectfully submitted,

THE STANDING COMMITTEE OF THE DIOCESE OF NEW YORK

Ellen was approved by the Standing Committee and the date of her ordination as deacon was set. In the meantime, a former Episcopal priest who had broken away from the Church in the 1960s to form his own rigidly conservative church found out about the ordination and sent a press release to the news services across the country. Because of this I had several telegrams asking me to desist, but no major eruption occurred. Naturally, I was concerned about what might happen. But when I called a special meeting of the Standing Committee and asked whether I should reconsider, the president said, "Don't you dare!"

Ellen's ordination to the diaconate took place quietly and with dignity on December 15, 1975, as described in the Prologue.

6

Sex Is a Dangerous Thing

The General Convention of the Episcopal Church in 1976 voted yes to the ordination of women to the priesthood and began to face openly the issue of homosexuality for the first time. We bishops and delegates to that convention were full of unsettled feelings and attitudes resulting from the changes of the past fifty years. All of us had lived through the sixties and, depending on our age, the part of the country where we lived, and whether we had older children, we had experienced different events and had changed in various ways. There had not been time enough for the culture in general, much less the Church, to absorb, consolidate, and indeed reach a consensus concerning these new attitudes. So much had happened so fast since most of us were children.

Fifty years seems a very short time in history, and yet in the last fifty years conventional morality concerning sex has changed more than in the last fifteen hundred years. When I was a child it was the only subject that was not discussed at all, ever. And yet I sensed that it was one of the most important subjects of all. Was it, I wondered, because the physical processes of the body were not particularly attractive? After all, people talked about throwing up and diarrhea . . . not at the dinner table to be sure, but elsewhere. Could it be somehow dangerous? I sensed danger, but other dangers were talked about because they *were* dangerous. My father never let us even point a stick at each other in mimic warfare, for fear that someday we would inadvertently point a loaded gun at someone. My sisters and brother and I were drowned by safety rules before we ever got to the ocean. What was this strange taboo, this fascinating, evil, dangerous, funny sex?

Since it was unthinkable to ask the adults about it, we were left to speculating about sex behind the barn, in the bathroom, and over forbidden cigarettes. I remember one conversation when I was about eight in which we seriously entertained the notion that the man urinated into the woman in order to produce children. A game we played was looking up sexy words in the dictionary, although dictionaries were censored in those days to prevent just such dangers. A friend of mine suggested we look up the word "friction," because he had just heard it was a sexy word. Sure enough, we looked it up: "the rubbing of one body against another."

No wonder strange beliefs and fears clustered around the subject of sex in the 1930s. Even in the 1950s, children were not much better informed. I remember one of the girls in my first parish church in Jersey City telling my wife that she was frightened about her wedding night. We thought this strange, since she had already had a baby by the young man she planned to marry. But she said she had heard that terrible things happened to you on your wedding night!

During the 1960s it was thought to be "modern" and sensible to talk to children about sex. However, the means of this communication were not always exactly relaxed.

In our parish in Jersey City, we decided that the teenagers needed a sex talk, as it was called in those days. We summoned a college friend who had just earned his medical degree in New York. It was a marvelous scene. He wore a three-piece suit, and sat bolt upright in a wing chair, while the youngsters in their satin jackets and blue jeans lounged in groups on the floor.

"Good evening boys and girls," he said. "It's nice to see you. Heh-heh. I, er, was asked to come here to your, er, uh, pretty little church by Father Moore. He thought you might like to hear a little bit about, er, ah, sex. Would you?"

Dead silence . . . not even a giggle.

"Well, er, uh, sex is very important, don't you think?"

Silence.

"It sure is. I mean, none of us would be here if it wasn't for good old sex, heh! heh!" he continued.

I counted two sickly grins in the audience.

"Well, let's get down to brass tacks. Each one of you boys has a . . . a . . . a . . ." He blushed a very deep red, and finally blurted out, "peter."

At that I left the room. The embarrassment level had overwhelmed me.

My generation was not particularly comfortable about sex. In the culture in which I grew up, knowledge of this kind was communicated, if at all, with the kind of emotion that distorted the content either with the prurient excitement of an adolescent or the anxiety of an adult. Furthermore, you never saw a person of the opposite sex naked, nor, at least in my experience, did boys talk with girls about such things. A fairly large percentage of my college class were virgins, and if they were not, their only experience was likely to have been with prostitutes. "Nice" girls did not "go all the way."

For a young man like me with serious religious convictions, the principle of celibacy outside marriage fitted with this rather puritanical upbringing. The traditional teaching of the Church learned at seminary substantiated this. And I must say, there was a logic about it. If you were unfortunate enough to be single, the Christian vocation was celibacy. You were to accept this "cross" as part of your life and gladly make the sacrifice like a good monk until you married. However, if someone had the misfortune to be divorced, he or she was condemned to a lifetime of celibacy. But, as a young married seminarian, I did not have to face that austere and sterile life myself.

Meanwhile, my experience and intuition were teaching me very different things. My own sexuality was a strong and important part of my being. Despite the fact that my school-teachers and Sunday school teachers said that sex was a God-given part of ourselves and therefore good, the more subtle message said that bodily desires were really sinful. St. Paul's admonition "It is better to marry than burn" was anything but constructive. The phrase "sinful desires of the flesh" seemed to mean that all desires of the flesh were sinful and, therefore, to be rejected, rather than the true meaning, which was that we were to reject those desires of the flesh which happened to be sinful.

I sensed that there was a dualistic view of sexuality which was the accepted standard of those around me. In other words, man was made up of flesh and spirit and the one was fighting against the other. God was on the side of the spirit, and the devil was on the side of the flesh. Now this is a clear and logical kind of belief to hold. It satisfies the puritan mind. It substantiates the guilt of a generation brought up in the repressive atmosphere which I had known. It colored much of the devotional literature which I read and the spiritual combat engaged in by many of the saints. One priest I knew suggested to his penitents that they could prevent masturbation by hanging on to the bedstead with both hands until they went to sleep.

However, part of me was sensing that this did not really make sense. In the Marine Corps I got to know men of great courage and integrity who were hardly puritans. At seminary I was beginning to have an understanding of the doctrines of the Creation and the Incarnation. God indeed had created us in all our physical nature. How then could such a powerful part of this nature be evil? And if God took on human flesh in the Incarnation, therefore Jesus Himself must have had these strong desires, although He apparently never married.

One summer at seminary I took a clinical training course and was exposed to Freudianism. This was a three-month program to give seminary students experience in hospital work and some psychiatric insights which would assist them in counseling and other pastoral work. We trained in general hospitals and mental hospitals as well as in a few prisons. I was told that the most intense and useful experience was in mental hospitals, so I chose Greystone, a huge old state hospital near Morristown, New Jersey, where my parents lived.

Despite the hospital chaplain's attempts to reconcile Freudianism and Christianity, most of us were confused by what we were hearing and seeing in the hospital and what we had learned in seminary. The Episcopal students were better off than the Methodist students, however, because our faith does not depend as heavily as theirs on religious emotional experience as the test of that faith. Thus we had a better intellectual and theological framework with which to deal with the trauma of being exposed for the first time to disturbed and psychotic patients. Nonetheless, we were shaken.

During the first six weeks of the program, I felt as if my own psychic underpinnings were about to give way. I was trying to stay afloat on a slippery log. The dynamics of mental illness, explained in Freudian terms, could be traced to sexual dislocations in the unconscious. A strong psychosexual development was necessary for mental health. Relationships with the mother and the father, if distorted, led to psychological arrest on an immature sexual level. In men, homosexuality was often caused, the doctors said, by an overly protective and affectionate mother or a stern and distant father. In women, the reverse was true. We students talked about being accepted more than about being loved. When one of us seemed a bit outside the group he felt rejected, and it was up to us to bring him back by accepting him more, accepting him as he was. The chaplain used the non-directive technique for counseling, and usually turned the conversation around so that we were not talking about the patients but about our own feelings. No one said what he thought about something, but said what he *felt* about something. I asked for some time off from the hospital program when our second child was born. I was given leave not because they knew I was needed at home, but because it would be a "valuable experience" for me.

The general message we were absorbing at the hospital was salvation through healthy emotions based on normal sexuality. We felt we could become like one of the inmates if we did not have a healthy sex life. This meant that the "sacredness" of marriage did not seem relevant. You can imagine the impact this had on seminary students, especially the young Methodists, fresh out of small Methodist colleges. A couple of them left the ministry as a result, and others came under more and more strain as the summer progressed, because they were living at a Methodist seminary and still were clinging to the rules of conduct forbidding smoking, drinking, and any kind of sexual activity outside marriage.

The blowup came about a week before the term was over. My mother and father were away and we had their large house all to ourselves. My wife, Jenny, and I decided it was up to us to have a farewell party for the students and the chaplain. We stocked up on Coca-Cola and soda and cider. We bought songbooks, set up the croquet set and the badminton net. For Episcopalians, a party without even beer seemed incongruous and, to use that summer's jargon, filled us with anxiety!

They arrived sharply at five o'clock and were barely through the door when they announced in unison, "We have decided to try it."

"Try what?" I asked.

"Drinking!" they exclaimed.

"My God," we said.

Luckily, my parents had a large liquor closet as well as a large house, so out came the whiskey and the gin and a case of beer.

At 3 A.M. the party was still roaring. The chaplain had gone to sleep, and the only black member of the group was having a ball being "lynched" by tipsy Methodists. A bleary-eyed couple, much the worse for wear, reappeared from a dark room. The girl said, "I have finally accepted Bob." Accepted indeed!

I often wondered whether these future Methodist parsons were ever able to stuff it all back in the bottle after that night. The party made me realize what enormous pressures were on people who were trying to lead the respectable American life, especially when we entered the years of the sexual revolution.

A few years later, I was under a good deal of personal tension myself and decided to have some psychotherapy. Gradually, as I explored my childhood, my dreams, my feelings, depth psychology began to make sense in my own self-understanding. I was beginning to feel less judgmental about sexuality and to realize more and more how the repressions caused by family and environment distorted my emotional life. Sexual "sins" seemed less serious now that I understood their origins. The rather free sexual mores of many of the people I got to know in Jersey City often seemed healthier than the complicated frustrations of other, more worldly acquaintances. Nor did these people seem to offend against the commandment of love, as long as no one was being betrayed or hurt by their sexual acts. And yet I still believed that all sexual activity outside marriage was *per se* sinful. This conflict between my intuitive understanding and moral conviction continued. I held them in tension, but it became increasingly difficult.

I remember one instance which was particularly painful.

In Indianapolis, where I became dean of Christ Church Cathedral in 1957, I had become friends with a respectable, middle-aged man who had recently been divorced. After a few months of loneliness, he met the right woman and wanted to be married, but under the strict marriage canon of our Church in those days I could not marry them. They went to another, less strict Protestant church and were married. He brought his wife to church the next Sunday and sat proudly in the first pew. By some unfortunate coincidence, I had decided to preach on Christian marriage that morning. As I condemned from the pulpit those who married against the canons of the Episcopal Church, I caught the eye of my friend. He turned away from my gaze in disgust and betrayal. He left church without shaking hands and I never saw him again. I have never overcome a feeling of resentment at the moralism which made me preach such a sermon and turn this good man away from his Church.

Like most families, ours was not prepared for the sixties. I still do not understand what happened, whence came the power, the anger, the strange utopianism which in those days informed the youth of Czechoslovakia, Japan, Paris, Woodstock. In our life, it began with the Beatles' haircut in the mid-1960s. By 1974, the hair in our family was more or less normal again. The Vietnam War was over. The black power movement had run its course. The campuses were quiet. The Woodstock nation had disappeared. But one thing remained: the sexual revolution.

In the sixties, our children, one by one, established close relationships with lovers. These "sons-out-of-law" and "daughters-out-of-law" became part of the family. We referred to them as "consorts," a rather elegant name my wife invented for what appeared to be a rather inelegant situation. Were we being sensible in this acceptance of "living in sin," or were we being weak? I rather think we were being pragmatic. It was quite clear that our children were not going to break off these liaisons no matter what we said. What would have been broken was their relationship with us. Their peer support was total. Almost all their friends were in similar situations. We made sure that they knew the physical facts of life, that they knew about birth control. We were pleased that they were being faithful to one another, as far as we could ascertain. They were living away from home. They were grown up. What were we to do? Cut them off? So went our endless discussions with ourselves and with our friends who had similar situations in their families. I remember one clergy gathering where this subject had arisen in a discussion group of about fifteen Episcopal priests. The leader asked the other participants to raise their hands if any of their children were living with a lover. All but two hands went up.

Our fallback position was that when they visited us they would stay in separate rooms. Even that fell apart late one night in the Adirondacks where we were vacationing. Our family camp there has separate cabins. Some of our older children had arrived a day or so before we did. My wife and two of the younger children had gone ahead in another car, and when I arrived, exhausted, about midnight, Jenny told me that my son and his girl friend were together in another cabin. He was twenty-three and had been living with her in California for over a year. They were to be with us for a month. Perhaps we were too tired to fight it. Perhaps we knew that sooner or later this last rampart of respectability would crumble. Perhaps beneath it all we really did not object. We decided to let them stay together.

As the years have passed, such arrangements have come to seem natural. Two of the children are married and have their own children. Another has been with her "consort" for seven years. When I look back on the difficulties many of my contemporaries had in marriage and the tensions and hostilities of couples I have counseled, often arising from neurotic sexual responses, I cannot be sure that the old way was better or even more moral.

It is that very distinction which continues to bother me intellectually. The Church has had clear teaching about sexual morality for hundreds of years. But between the law of biblical morality and the working out of the commandment of love in a particular time and place there often seems to be a discrepancy. In the gospels, it would seem that Jesus came down on the side of love over law. When criticized for allowing His disciples to pick grain on the Sabbath, He quoted the Old Testament story in which David allowed his troops to eat the holy bread of the temple because they were hungry. When called to task for healing a man's withered arm on the Sabbath, Jesus asked the Pharisees whether they would not pull their ass out of a ditch on the Sabbath. "The Sabbath was made for man, not man for the Sabbath," He said. In other words, the law is an instrument of love, the servant of love. When the law goes against this higher commandment, it can be broken.

However, since the morality of the Bible and the Church has such a venerable tradition, one does not go against it lightly. And so I find myself becoming more and more sure in my own mind that flexibility in sexual morality is now indicated, but am not yet willing to say officially that this should be the Church's position.

Many, perhaps most, of the clergy who have received clinical training find themselves counseling one thing and yet unable to say that same thing from the pulpit. The Church is divided into two camps: one that follows what seems to be common sense under the commandment of love and human decency, and another that says that the law of the Bible and the teachings of the Church are immutable even when they seem to go against this common sense and compassion.

They feel that if that edifice is breached, the result will be moral anarchy, and that the world will become like Times Square or the late Roman Empire.

Like other great historic changes, the sexual revolution has proceeded on many fronts, and various institutions, not least the family, have changed in meeting the challenge. The women's movement grew out of a combination of the civil rights movement and the sexual revolution. The gay movement in turn followed the women's movement. In this historical context, the Episcopal Church was deciding whether women could be ordained and what it should think about homosexuality, an even more difficult issue.

7

Episcopalians by the Thousands

The General Convention of the Episcopal Church is a combination of legislature, reunion, eucharistic congress, political convention, job market, sideshow, and benefit. The convention is a bicameral legislature which meets every three years to enact legislation for governing the Church. There is one Presiding Bishop, who serves a twelve-year term, and approximately two hundred other bishops in a House of Bishops. A priest or layman is elected president of the House of Deputies at each convention, which includes more than a thousand clergy and lay representatives elected by each diocese of the Church.

The constitution of our Church was written by many of the same men who wrote the Constitution of the United States, thus the legislative procedure of the Church functions in the same bicameral fashion. Legislation can originate in either House but must be passed in both to become law. Amendments are offered in the usual manner, and joint committees iron out differences. For important pieces of legislation, public hearings are held. Each House has committees to deal with different areas of concern. For instance, committees on national and international affairs, on the ministry, liturgy, budget, and so forth. Some of the committees are

joint committees of both Houses, some are committees of
a particular House. This rather cumbersome process must
take place in ten working days.

The most recent convention descended on the city of Minneapolis in October 1976. It was to be a historic event because
the first of two readings needed to adopt the new prayer
book was to be voted on, as well as the ordination of women
to the priesthood. We all knew that the outcome of these
issues would alter the life of the Church for years to come.
I had been asked time and again what I would do if the
ordination of women was defeated. I could not answer because I simply did not know. What I did know was that my
own diocese would blow up whatever I did. If I ordained
against the law, the conservatives would be greatly upset.
If I refused, the women and their backers would be even
more upset. Whichever I did, the uneasy peace of the last
few years would be shattered. Many people felt that our
Church would cease to be a valid part of the Catholic Church
if women were priests. This meant they would leave the
Church. This kind of person cherished the Catholicity of
the Church, the fact that we were possessed of the apostolic
succession of bishops and the threefold ministry of bishops,
priests, and deacons coming down unbroken from the time
of the apostles. They felt ordaining women would be a break
with this Catholicity, and would literally destroy the validity
of the whole Church.

With some notable exceptions, it was liberals versus conservatives, and not the more traditional adversaries, those
of High Church versus Low Church. No one was sure who
were his allies. Neither did the lines divide between younger
and older persons, or between men and women. Thus no
one was sure which way the vote would go.

Since the Episcopal Church is a relatively small denomination, it cheers us to gather in such a large mass. To find a
small city stuffed with Episcopalians is bizarre but hearten-

ing—Episcopalians in lobbies, Episcopalians in restaurants, Episcopalians in beer joints, Episcopalians in buses; black Episcopalians, Oriental Episcopalians, Sunbelt Episcopalians, New England Episcopalians—all crawling around Minneapolis, of all places.

Minneapolis is a friendly city. We arrived on a Friday and were suitably welcomed over the weekend by various church groups. From Saturday night to Sunday afternoon the caucuses were busy lining up votes and determining strategy. Parties were held in honor of this or that, and position papers were prepared. On Monday evening I met with the New York delegates to the House of Deputies to discuss strategy on the women's issue. It was hard for us to concentrate because one of our delegates, Charles Lawrence, had been nominated for president of the House of Deputies at the next convention. Charles was black, a professor of sociology, and an advocate of civil rights causes in a persistent, low-key fashion. He and his wife, Margaret, were close friends of ours. I was just as excited about his possible election as about the issues. If elected, he would be the first black president of the House of Deputies. Both Charles's election and women's ordination were "liberal" causes and to some degree dependent on each other for acceptance by the convention.

My wife, Brenda, and I had lunch in our room on Wednesday, the afternoon of the vote on women priests. We had looked for bits of news in the local papers which would somehow point to the struggle ahead. As we walked out to the elevator we met several bishops who were against women's ordination, and we forced a happy smile. The elevator ride was long. We had nothing to say because there was everything to say. At times like that the devil makes me want to say outrageous things like: "How's your sex life, buddy?" Or, "Do you think Mae West would have made a good bishop . . . she's a member of St. Mary the Virgin on Forty-sixth Street, you know."

We walked from the hotel to the Minneapolis Convention Center where both Houses were meeting. Outside the bishops' hall we were stopped by lobbyists and well-wishers. "Good luck." "Give 'em hell." "I saw Bishop so-and-so, he really looked gloomy." "Go for a big majority, it will shove it over the top." I felt as though we were going into a football game!

The room was almost full when we arrived. I was organized a bit earlier than usual and glanced over the notes of a speech I intended to give if the debate needed my emphasis. I had been quieter in the House than was my custom, holding my fire for this issue. I had a terrible time being quiet, but in any assembly, if you speak too much you lose your effectiveness. Other bishops were at their seats shuffling papers. I looked over to the gallery and saw Brenda slip into one of the last vacant seats. The Presiding Bishop called for order, and we began with a reading from Scripture by, according to custom, one of the most recently elected bishops. I thought to myself, "What a way for a new bishop to start his life in the House of Bishops," facing this debate. The Presiding Bishop led us in prayer, the usual thing, asking for guidance from the Holy Spirit, but also praying for a conciliatory attitude. I really got into *that* prayer.

After a few announcements, Bishop Allin called for the special order of the day and talked about the conduct of debate, hoping that it would be on a high level, stating once more how much was at stake. He then called for the report of the Committee on the Ministry. The chairman, Bishop James Montgomery of Chicago went up to the podium.

Jim Montgomery is one of my oldest friends in the Church. We were classmates at seminary, and even then everyone knew that someday he would be Bishop of Chicago. He is bright, enormously fair, and has a quick smile. He grew up in Chicago, which is a traditionally High Church diocese, where he was involved in youth groups and acolyte guilds.

After seminary, he had a distinguished ministry as a parish priest. Jim had never married. His whole life was devoted to the Church. But unlike many Anglo-Catholics, he was not rigid and had a strong social conscience. However, he could not bring himself to endorse the ordination of women. He was in an embarrassing position as he reported on the resolution in favor of ordination.

The original wording of the resolution was complicated. It said, in effect, that women could be ordained to the priesthood in those dioceses which were in favor of it. Numerous "whereases" having to do with conscience and diocesan prerogatives preceded the "Be it resolved . . ."

The initial debate was aimed at clarifying the wording, which was, in a sense, a compromise. Finally it became clear that both conservatives and liberals wanted to go for broke. The resolution was amended to state simply that the canons on ordination were to be interpreted as permitting women as well as men to be ordained.

Now we had the issue ready for debate. Although every one of us had heard all the arguments many times before, this was the first time the issue was before us for action, and not merely for our opinion or for a "mind of the House" resolution. It seemed appropriate, therefore, for the arguments to be formally on parade one last time.

Those who were against stated their side: Jesus had not chosen women apostles. Since He was a social radical for His time, He would have chosen women apostles if He had thought that women should be successors to the apostles, despite the prevailing patriarchal culture. (The resolution opened the office of bishop—the apostolic succession—to women as well as the office of priest.) The opposition countered that Jesus needed the most effective leaders for His mission and that a woman in those days simply could not carry out the kind of assignment the apostles were given. Furthermore, Jesus had said that the Holy Spirit would reveal truths later on which the Church was not then ready to hear. Ordaining women was a case in point. It took the Church eighteen hundred years to realize slavery was un-Christian, so length of time makes no difference.

Another classic argument was that since a priest takes the role of Jesus at the altar, and Jesus was a man, therefore the priest must be a man. The opposing argument was that Saint John said that the Word became flesh and dwelt among us. Jesus took on all humanity in his incarnation, not just men. Therefore any human being can be the celebrant of the Eucharist. Furthermore, if we believe in the "priesthood of all believers," women already have a priestly function.

But God the Father is masculine. The Creator is an active, masculine force. The female identity is passive and receiving. Therefore a woman priest will distort the image of God. This argument brought exclamations of "Stereotype," "High time the image of God included both sexes," and "An image beyond sexuality."

One of the bishops who had been most active in ecumenical conversations with the Roman Catholic Church stated that the ordination of women would not only be a setback in these conversations, but would perhaps end them. "We should wait," he said, "until the whole Church, all the Churches, can settle the issue together." The rejoinder: "But this may not happen for centuries. If it is the right thing to do, we should lead the way. Furthermore, my brothers, you may have noticed a telegram on each one of our desks from a Roman Catholic group representing thousands of nuns, urging us to approve women's ordination."

Finally I could keep quiet no longer. I went to the podium to speak to the issue in terms of the missionary role of the Church in this time of history. Most New Yorkers are more chauvinistic about their hometown than the most Babbitt-like Midwestern chamber of commerce member, even though we tend to hide it under a layer of urbanity several inches thick. But most of us feel that in New York you tend to find today what you will find in the rest of the country tomorrow. For good and ill, New York is a symbol of the future. Certainly we work in a cultural milieu far different from that of the South or the West. In order to minister in New York, where the women's liberation movement began, and in order to portray the Church as alert and concerned, we need to translate our teaching more quickly to the temper of the times than does the Church in other parts of the country. In New York many of the people with whom I worked took for granted the basic tenets of women's liberation and simply could not understand the theological niceties which prevented women from being ordained. In their eyes this was an instance of the Church standing in the way of justice. Thus the gospel expressed in male chauvinist actions was "bad news" in New York, not "good news."

"We have talked for years about the subject before us today," I began. "There have been many issues on which the Anglican Church and the Episcopal Church have taken the lead, and I feel we have a vocation here today of leadership rather than of consensus.

"This afternoon I would like to talk about the missionary implications of the decision we make today. I think of myself as a missionary bishop; in that sense as an apostle. I think of the Church as an instrument of God in the world. I feel we are most truly the Church when we are looking outward toward God's people outside our Church. You know as well as I do, my brothers and sisters, that there is a crisis in mission. Therefore we should be considering our missionary strategy, perhaps more than anything else in this convention, and we are not. You may say the Church is the Body of Christ; we must be sure that it is correct and orderly and clean. I remind you that our Lord Jesus Christ, Himself, thought of Himself as an instrument and was willing to be made dirty, and willing to be broken, in order that the world might be redeemed. I am willing for our Church to break some small parts of its order; I am willing for our Church to take the leadership, amongst the so-called Catholic churches; I am willing to accept some inconsistencies of the kind which have been mentioned today; I am willing, even, for us to be broken, if this is the only way by which we may be an instrument to redeem our brothers and our sisters in the world.

"Believe me, where I live the decision we make today will radically affect the social mission of the Church and the evangelism of the Church. Few will take my words seriously about the plight of the poor in New York City or any other social issue, if our Church turns inward in fear today. As for evangelism, many of the young people whom I know through my nine children, my six daughters, are already laughing at our antics. God help us with such young persons if we do not make it possible today for the young women of our Church to seek the priesthood if they feel a vocation.

"The people who are not Christians; the people—the thousands, the millions, in our cities and all over our land—look at the image of any institution in rather broad terms, without all the details filled in. I want them to see our Church as an open, expanding, welcoming, joyful Church, full of accepting love for all of God's people, opening its doors wide," (I spread my long arms as wide as I could) "being able to accept any of God's people who are called to a full, glorious priesthood. There should be no question that we are reflecting the image of our Lord Jesus Christ, His openness and His joy in all His children."

As soon as I sat down, the Bishop of Northern California, one of the staunchest conservatives in the House, arose and, to the amusement of everyone including myself, said, "I think that no matter how wide the Bishop of New York spreads his mighty arms, women priests will not bring the people of New York streaming into his churches."

The debate continued for two hours more, and when the vote was taken, the resolution easily passed the House of Bishops. About twenty bishops voted no and registered their negative vote with the secretary.

The vote was not a total surprise, but because there were some new bishops in the House since the last year's vote, and because the political pressure had mounted enough to make some bishops change their minds to the extent of abstaining, we were right to have been a bit concerned. Now, however, the resolution went to the House of Deputies, where the outcome was most uncertain. At the convention three years before, the resolution had originated in that House and had been defeated summarily. After three years and an enormous amount of discussion in the Church, we felt very hopeful.

Since the debate in the House of Deputies took place during our own legislative time I did not hear it, but I was told that it followed the same lines as the debate in the House of Bishops. We adjourned just in time to go to the House of Deputies for the historic vote. This was September 16, 1976.

Resolved, the House of Deputies concurring, that a new Section 1 of Title III, Canon 9 be adopted, with renumbering of the present Section 1 and following, the said Section 1 to read as follows:
Section 1: The provision of these canons for the admission of Candidates, and for the Ordination to the three Orders, Bishops, Priests, and Deacons, shall be equally applicable to men and women.

The Reverend John Coburn, rector of St. James' Church in New York and now Bishop-elect of Massachusetts, was in the chair as president of the House of Deputies. He had delayed his actual consecration as bishop so that he could preside over this important session. He was a masterful chairman, firm, quiet, reasonable, and humorous. Shepherding this particular bit of legislation and chairing the debate tested his abilities. He knew that the way the issue was dealt with would be almost as important as its outcome. Bitter rancor and disorder were to be avoided at all costs.

"My friends, fellow deputies, and members of the gallery," John Coburn began, "we now come to a solemn moment in the life of our Church which will affect its course in the years to come. The matter has been debated fairly and well. Before asking for the vote, may I request that we keep five minutes of silence during which we will ask for the guidance of God's Holy Spirit."

The deputies' hall was a huge amphitheater which could have housed a football field. It must have been fifty feet up to the steel girders which supported the ceiling, and at least three hundred feet square. The chairman and his assistants sat on a raised platform at one end of the hall. Facing them were row after row of seats, almost a thousand, where the delegates representing all the dioceses of the Church were seated. Each delegation had a sign above its section: Florida, Washington, New York, Alaska, Ecuador, etc. At first glance it looked like the nominating convention of a political party. Alongside the delegates' stations and separated by a low barricade and aisles were bleachers for the gallery, twenty rows high. At this moment, every seat was filled and the open spaces by the doors were full of people standing. The hall reverberated with excited conversation. But when John called for silence it was as if not one person was even breathing.

I have never heard such an awesome silence; immense, tension-filled, Spirit-filled. Five minutes is a long time to be silent in such a place. I bowed my head and prayed earnestly for the guidance of the Spirit, that justice be done, that the Church remain at unity with herself. And I prayed for all the women of our Church whose lives would be affected so much by the next few minutes, for those who had waited patiently and for those who had taken matters into their own hands by being ordained illegally in Philadelphia. I thought of them, one by one. I remembered the phone call in Venice when Bishop DeWitt told me he was going ahead with the Philadelphia ordination. And I remembered the service at our cathedral when the women knelt before me and looked up with pleading eyes. The silence continued. I opened my eyes and looked out across that hall full of people, wondering what they were thinking. I thought it was an improbable place for this decision to occur.

"Amen!" John Coburn said loudly and firmly. "We will now begin the balloting by orders." Each delegation had one vote for the clergy and one vote for the lay delegates. The clergy and lay votes were counted separately, but a majority in each order was necessary for passage. If the vote of the four clergy or lay persons in a delegation was tied two to two, the vote did not count. In that instance, their vote amounted to a "no" vote. So there had to be more than a majority of all clergy and all lay persons for the resolution to pass.

The chair called for a recess during the counting of the ballots. The hall was filled with noisy speculation and nervous laughter for about twenty minutes. Like the silence, it seemed endless. Finally the chair called the House to order and asked the secretary to read the result.

"Clerical votes: one hundred and fourteen votes cast, fifty-eight needed for affirmative action. Sixty votes yes; thirty-nine votes no; fifteen votes divided.

"Lay votes: one hundred thirteen votes cast, fifty-seven votes needed for affirmative action. Sixty-four votes yes; thirty-six votes no; thirteen votes divided. The resolution carried in both orders."

Immediately, the chair called upon the chaplain to lead the House in prayer. As soon as the prayer concluded, the chair recognized the Reverend Kenneth Trueman of the Diocese of Milwaukee, who read a statement saying that he could not with good conscience accept the action of the House, but that he intended to stay within the life of the Church; that he could not accept the authority of the Episcopal Church in such a grave matter acting separately from the Orthodox and Roman Catholic Church; that this action brought under serious question the position of our Church as a Catholic and apostolic body. All who wished to sign the statement were advised to do so. The House adjourned at 6:45 P.M.

There was no cheering and no groaning for the vote or for Trueman's statement. Instead, a rather wonderful thing happened. I saw deputies whom I knew to have voted on opposite sides of the question rush over to one another to shake hands, to embrace. Nearly everyone's eyes were filled with tears. I sought out a priest in our delegation, an old and dear friend, who had opposed the ordination of women strongly. We held each other for a moment or two, and we cried.

If only, I thought, this spirit of reconciliation could continue.

The rest of the convention, of course, was anticlimactic. We had a debate in the House of Bishops as to whether to recognize the irregularly ordained women. After much feeling had been expressed, the bishops of the dioceses to which the women belonged, such as New York, prevailed upon the House to allow a service of recognition rather than a conditional ordination as the method by which to receive the women as priests. This preserved the conscience of those who believed that they had been ordained in Philadelphia, but allowed for the needed canonical validation in a formal eucharistic setting.

8

Women in the Kingdom

To kneel before a bishop, to feel the weight of his hands upon your head, to hear the ancient words "Receive the Holy Ghost for the Office and Work of a Priest in the Church of God, now committed unto thee by the imposition of our hands," is to be permanently changed. You feel the power of the Holy Spirit, so it seems, entering your nerves, entering your mind, filling the innermost crevices of your unconscious. At that moment body, mind, emotion, spirit, soul, are open, vulnerable, alert. The moment of ordination is one over which you have prayed and prayed, whether kneeling before God in a monastery in the dead of night or at a crowded altar rail on a Sunday morning. Like marriage, it is an irrevocable act which can never be completely undone.

I have spent many long hours discussing what the theology of ordination might be, especially with clergy who work in the secular world. Some, who lean toward a theological perspective of a Catholic kind, think the sacrament of holy orders is indelible. Using the philosophical categories of Thomas Aquinas, which he inherited from Aristotle, they would say a person's character is permanently changed. Others, more Protestant in their theology, would stress the blessing of a vocation, or inner call. Still others would take a view that the function of the person is the important thing, and that ordination gives official approval to particular kinds of ministry: hearing confessions and stating God's forgiveness, blessing the sick, presiding at the Eucharist. However, no matter how functional, no matter how subjective their particular theology of ordination might be, priests have a strong possessiveness about their ordination.

I remember a conversation with a group of clergy in the Diocese of Washington, D.C., in which I was pushing hard for a minimum standard of behavior for an ordained priest working in the world. One in the group, who was extremely liberal and Protestant in his views, kept denying anything unique about a priest, saying that a priest did not have to celebrate the Eucharist, or preach, or baptize in order to exercise his priesthood. "Well, then," I said, "Why don't you resign your active ministry?"

"No, no," he said, startled. "I can't do that. It's part of who I am."

In the days before psychology, this experience of permanent change at ordination was expressed theologically by such doctrines as "indelibility." Depth psychology has provided other names for the experience. However you describe it, ordination is a traumatic experience so deep and important that you can never be the same afterward. Written into our canon law is the principle that no one can be ordained more than once. If a person should lose his faith and resign from the active ministry, or if because of a grave moral offense should be deposed from the ministry, and at a later time wish to be reinstated, the ceremony does not include the "laying on of hands," or any reordination. By the same token, if a priest of the Roman Catholic Church is received into our Church and wishes to exercise his priesthood, he is received as a priest, not reordained.

Earlier I described how my old friend John, a deposed priest, continued acting like a priest during his long years of mental illness and alcoholism. A classic fictional account of the same phenomenon is Graham Greene's *The Power and the Glory,* in which he describes a "whiskey priest" in Mexico who continued to martyrdom despite his less than admirable character. Nothing upsets me more than the plight of the unemployed clergy in my diocese who, because of the present economy, cannot find jobs, Often, it is almost impossible for them to look for jobs outside the Church with any enthusiasm, so deep is their dedication to priesthood.

I took nine years to decide to seek my own ordination. I felt unworthy, enormously unworthy. Imagine always, *always* having people know you are a priest and holding you to a higher standard of behavior. Think of having to curb your language (a problem I have still!), of having to be careful of your life style, of really never being free again to act without regard to your priestliness. How hard it would be, I thought, to have to love everyone, at least to the point of serving them whether you liked them or not. And to live a life completely dependent on a belief in God, a belief which, so I thought, could easily disappear. But above all, how presumptuous to put on the symbolic robes of Christ, to stand before the altar in His role, and to say those terrible words, "This is my Body which is given for you, This is my Blood which is shed for you"; to see your own hands which have touched so many things, touching the holy Bread. An impossible responsibility because you have to do it morning after morning, no matter whether you feel like it or not, no matter what sin you may have committed. Bad enough to have to repeat those liturgical words, but then the preaching; no matter your own state of belief or morale or depression, you have to stand up and preach the Word of God in confidence and joy. I remember bursting into tears when I made my confession the night before I was consecrated bishop. It just seemed too much, too much.

Whatever the professionalism of the ministry, you can be sure that for most persons ordination is at least as deep an experience as marriage. And for the bishop ordaining, the moment is unlike any other experience. Religious emotion, religious sensitivity, is difficult to isolate. You are never completely sure what is imagination and what is the strong real presence of the force of God in your life. Nonetheless, when the experience affects the course of your life, it attains a solemnity stronger than other, more passionate feelings. To describe such an event, when an objective occurrence and inward feeling coincide, is subject to misinterpretation. What I can say is that all these emotions and anxieties, the expectation and excitement, were present as I prepared for the first ordination in our diocese of a woman to the priesthood. I was also aware of the historic significance of the moment for the diocese and for me personally. I could not believe that finally I would say the holy words of ordination as I laid my hands on the head of a woman.

On January 9, 1977, Sister Mary Michael Simpson was the ordinand at my first woman's ordination. She had been for many years, and still is, a nun in the Episcopal Order of St. Helena. She taught school, did missionary work in Liberia, and had become a lay therapist. She has a small office over my office in New York, where she counsels clients of all kinds. Mary Michael is a most confident, no-nonsense person of real strength and maturity. She is happy in her religious vocation, she feels secure in her work as a psychologist, but has a valid vocation to priesthood as well. I can think of no one about whom I could be more sure that this was the right step. She has a kindly, strong face, dark red hair, a professional air about her. As far as I know, she was to be the first nun in the history of the Church to be made a priest.

Not only was Mary Michael to be ordained that night, but Carter Heyward, who was ordained illegally in Philadelphia, had asked to be regularized at the same service.

The service was in the evening at the high altar above the great choir in the Cathedral of St. John the Divine. The choir, which seats about three hundred people, was full. The lighting made the candles sparkle, and the gold embroidery on the altar cloth shone warmly as a background for the ceremony. From where I would sit, in front of the altar, the huge nave disappeared into darkness behind the circle of light in the choir, and the red marble pillars stretched up strong around us toward an invisible ceiling.

The formal procession of clergy, acolytes, Mary Michael, and Carter Heyward, as well as those who were to present them, proceeded along the ambulatory which surrounds the great choir. As we walked through the dark space I felt a strong emotion building up within me. I was at the end of the procession, in cope and miter, carrying my bishop's staff and feeling very alone and slightly disengaged from the moment. Inside I felt pressure. I could not tell if it was excitement or grief or anger. I could not tell if it was deep joy at Mary Michael's ordination, or residual anger at Carter Heyward's behavior toward me, or total relief that Carter and I no longer had to be in conflict. It was, perhaps, a combination of all these things.

We came through the opening and into the brightness, took our positions, waited for the organ to stop its rumbling. Carter came forward. She is a small person with large eyes. A fighter. This was the consummation of her long struggle to be a priest. As she stood in the presence of God, in front of His altar, a mixture of triumph and humility seemed to play over her face. She looked very, very small as she stood there in that space in front of where I was sitting at the top of the steps.

"Carter," I said, "we have been through a lot together. We have been closely bound together by a common passion for justice. We have been separated by the way of attaining that justice. The separation has often seemed like betrayal. You have hurt me, wounded me. I am sure I have wounded you. But now, thank God, we are to forgive one another and ask the forgiveness of God Himself for whatever sins we have committed in conflict. And I want you to know that over the past years I have always respected your integrity and admired your courage." The emotion started to force its way out of my chest. I paused to fight it back. My chin stuck out. My lips quivered. ". . . and I . . . am very fond of . . . you." And then it came, a flood of tears which I could not control. I am not embarrassed at showing emotion, but this was too much. I just stood there unable to control my feelings. I let the tears flow until they ceased, reached into my sleeve for a handkerchief, snuffled a bit. Loyalties, betrayals, anger, sorrow. Now joy and relief. It all came flooding out.

I continued, "The experience we are having is an experience of Grace, for it is illogical that the very hurts, indeed the very sins with which we have been separated, when forgiven, when healed, are transformed by Jesus into love, active love. And so we welcome Carter into our midst today with great joy, with great love.

"There is still much work to do," I said. "Ordained women are still denied recognition. We pledge ourselves to continue the struggle together.

"Let us confess our sins against God and our neighbor, and especially our sinfulness in the oppression of women in the life of the Church and the world, and in the wounds inflicted upon one another."

We knelt in silence together for a time. Then said slowly:

> Most merciful God,
> we confess that we have sinned against you
> in thought, word and deed,
> by what we have done,
> and by what we have left undone.
> We have not loved you with our whole heart;
> we have not loved our neighbors as ourselves.
> We are truly sorry and we humbly repent.
> For the sake of your Son Jesus Christ,
> have mercy on us and forgive us;

> that we may delight in your will,
> and walk in your ways,
> to the glory of your Name.   Amen.

I stood up to declare the Absolution:

Almighty God have mercy on you, forgive you all your sins through our Lord Jesus Christ, strengthen you in all goodness, and by the power of the Holy Spirit keep you in eternal life. Amen.

I looked Carter full in the face and solemnly declared: "Carter, on July 29, 1974, you took the Oath of Conformity and were ordained a priest in the Church of God. You have been recommended to that order by the Bishop and the Standing Committee of this diocese, and whereas the Sixty-fifth General Convention of the Episcopal Church has resolved that women may be ordained to the priesthood in the Episcopal Church, therefore, we welcome you as a priest in good standing of the Diocese of New York and of the Episcopal Church in the United States of America."

I stepped forward, took Carter by the hand, and received her as a priest in good standing. The short liturgy over, I embraced her and a few more tears filled my eyes and hers. The congregation clapped loudly. Many of them had been in the struggle from the beginning. It was a victory for us all.

A hymn played and we began the liturgy for the ordination of Sister Mary Michael. The feelings aroused by her ordination were far different from the mounting tension and tearful relief I'd felt at Carter's regularization. Here, instead, was the flowering of a long and steady vocation, taken a step at a time under the regular canonical process of the Church. I went to the lectern to preach.

"This," I said, "is a most historic moment. For the first time in the history of the Holy Catholic Church we gather to lay hands on a nun for the office of priest in the Church of God. We welcome you all, and especially the sisters from the Roman Catholic Church who are here to lend their prayers and support.

"Women were the first to embrace the religious life. The New Testament speaks of the widows and virgins who chose this special way of serving their Lord. Macrina, Sister of Gregory of Nyssa, started the first monastic community. Women joined the desert fathers of St. Anthony. Pachomius mentions communities of women in his account of the first monastic communities. The history of prayer, of sanctity, of martyrdom, is filled with the glories of women saints, women religious.

"Today, late in the course of time, we take a giant step, the opening up of the priesthood to this heritage of the past, this enormous potential for the future. There are those who say that a woman cannot be a priest. In a sense they are right, no human being can be a priest in and of him or herself. We believe that Christ alone is the great high priest and that all priesthood derives from Him. He made the one, true, pure, immortal sacrifice, He alone is worthy to stand as a mediator between God and man. Our priesthood only exists as an extension of His.

"The Church as a whole is His Body and as a whole exercises His priesthood here and now. This is the meaning of the phrase, the 'priesthood of all believers.' Women, as members of the Church, are *already* priests in this sense. Therefore, there can be no metaphysical or essential barrier to their priesthood. Ordained priesthood is an ordering of the priesthood of all belivers, giving to certain persons the responsibility of being the representatives of this priesthood. In ordering the instrumentality of this holy corporate priesthood there are different vocations. What we are doing and saying today is that response to these different vocations is not limited by sex any more than it is limited by nationality or race.

"I *feel* this to be true; I *know* this to be true. I have sensed this vocation deep in the hearts of Mary Michael and Carter, and of many other women. The Word became *flesh* and dwelt among us. Christ took on all humanity, not mere maleness. It has taken us so long to understand! 'In Christ is neither Jew nor Greek, male nor female.' In Christ's priesthood there is neither Jew nor Greek, black nor white, male nor female.

"God reveals His will over the years, reveals Himself, His nature gradually. The story of the Bible is the story of God revealing Himself to man when man has been able to comprehend the revelation. And the revelation is always from small to larger, from slavery to freedom. Our personal God is always too small. God as He is is too large for us. He continues to force us to understand the scope of His Being. Consider these times of revelation:

"First: Jahweh was thought to be the God only of Israel in the early days of that desert people. Through the exile in Babylon, He forced them to realize He was the God of the whole earth.

"Second: In the Old Testament of Jesus' day, He was thought of as a God of narrow law. Jesus forced us through His own death upon the Cross to realize Him to be a God of love far beyond the compassion of the law.

"Third: St. Paul, by his witnessing of the Holy Spirit coming to the Gentiles with whom he worked, was forced to understand that Christ was the Saviour of the Gentiles and not the Saviour only of the Jews.

"Fourth: The Reformation leaders returned the Bible to all men and gave them back their consciences.

"Last: Today, late in time, we have been forced by the work of God in the women's liberation movement to see that the ordained priesthood is open to all persons, not just men. What a marvelous Epiphany, what a marvelous breakthrough!

"I remember sitting in this very cathedral not many months ago as women ordinands knelt before me and feeling that my hands were tied behind my back. I struggled to loosen them. Today they are free to lay upon a woman's head.

"We open the priesthood to the flood of love God has given the world through the feminine, through the spiritual power of religious women.

"There is much still to do. This is but the first step in what will be a long, often painful, and dreary task of having the Church fully opened up to the ministry of women."

It is customary, at the end of an ordination sermon, to give a charge to the ordinand. For this the ordinand stands.

"Mary Michael, to this task you are called. To this task and indeed to the whole task of your priesthood you bring not only yourself but the strength of your whole community, the Order of St. Helena. You bring to this task the balance and discipline of the religious life, the internal certainty of prayer, and the perseverance brought by prayer. Our Church, our priesthood, sorely needs these gifts in the years ahead.

"Remember, however, first and foremost you are a priest in the Church of God. Like any other priest, pick up your Cross and follow Him."

Finally Mary Michael knelt before the bishop's chair and the other priests clustered around and put their hands, together with mine, on her head. "Receive the Holy Ghost," I said in solemn voice, "for the Office and Work of a Priest in the Church of God. . . ." It seemed so natural, and it also seemed natural to kneel down after the service to receive her blessing. How could this quiet act have caused such controversy?

The time came to ordain Ellen Barrett. Naïvely, I thought that with all the excitement over the other women, Ellen would receive little publicity. Her ordination to the diaconate having attracted little attention, I assumed that not much notice would be given to this event. I had not taken into account the media's need to keep a story going. This event was a natural. Women were being ordained, now a so-called lesbian was to be ordained. On January 6, 1977, an article appeared in the New York *Post* which was typical:

An avowed lesbian will be among thirty women entering the Episcopal priesthood this month.

Ellen Marie Barrett, thirty years of age, now working on a doctorate in social ethics at the Graduate Theological Union in Berkeley, California, will be ordained here Monday night by Bishop Paul Moore, the Episcopal Bishop of New York.

Miss Barrett will be only the second publicly known homosexual to be ordained to the clergy by a major Christian denomination in recent years. The Rev. William Johnson was ordained a United Church of Christ minister in 1972, by an association of UCC churches in the San Francisco Bay area.

Miss Barrett said she didn't think her sexual orientation would create much additional controversy in the three million member church. . . .

Letters and telegrams began to come to my home and office, all demanding that I cease and desist:

For the sake of the Church I urge you not to ordain a lesbian. Your impatient action is further disregard for lawful procedure and will cause additional suffering and laceration of the Church.

Clarence R. Haden
Bishop of Northern California
January 8, 1977

Dear Paul, our phone is busy today. Clergy and laity protesting your proposed ordination of a lesbian to the priesthood. This hurts the whole Church. To be personal, I shall be sharing the priesthood with a lesbian. Is this fair? I know I am a sinner, but have never tried to make a virtue of sin. Please don't hurt the Church any more.

Charles Persell
Bishop of Albany
January 7, 1977

Please, please do not go through with the ordination on Monday. Ordination of practicing homosexuals does not, underline not, represent the mind of the Church, and is plainly contrary to the teaching of scripture which we have all been sworn to uphold. There are far more constructive ways to show pastoral concern for homosexuals than by attempting to bless that which God offers to redeem. Paul, you cannot imagine the tremendous harm you are doing to the rest of the Church. At the very least please show consideration to those homosexuals who are seeking more positive solutions to their difficulties, and who will be hurt by the inevitable reaction to this ordination. It pains me to write this to a trusted friend, but I must. Your proposed action appears to be totally irresponsible.

> William C. Frey
> Bishop of Colorado
> January 7, 1977

And the following was received from a psychologist:

The depressing announcement of your presumptuous decision to ordain a self-advertised, aggressive female deviate into the Episcopal priesthood throws further doubt shared nationwide on the direction and inner strength of the Episcopal Church. As you must know, the Episcopal priesthood already has more than its share of individuals showing traits of sexual instability. You must also know that openly professed homosexuals are usually the missionary type who often actually proselytize others into their unhappy unnatural ways of life, highly offensive to all normal people whether Episcopalian or not. For a Bishop of the Episcopal Church to take part in this sordid sad story can only add to the increasing despair of an already fractured Church. May God forgive you, Bishop Moore.

The little Church of the Holy Apostles where Ellen was to be ordained was in the center of the storm. The young rector and his vestry were doing their best, but began to be overwhelmed. Three television networks wanted to broadcast the event live. Other media demanded a press conference. We decided to let one television camera in, and to set up a press conference after the service for Ellen and another woman who was to be ordained at the same time, Annette Ruark. Stuart Wetmore, my suffragan bishop, said,

"Paul, this is going to be the biggest explosion yet." He was right. The signs were ominous.

Brenda and I drove downtown in bitter cold and snow to the church. We saw television trucks and police cars. Someone led us through the confusion to the rector's office, where I would vest. We all were anxious. I had been told that objections to the ordination would be made at the service. I worried that someone might try to stop the service.

It was something of a circus, with reporters there in numbers and the congregation rubber-necking to see the television camera. After a few minutes, however, the prayers began and we settled into the solemn drama of ordination. We came to the place in the service where objections could be made:

Dear Friends in Christ, you know the importance of this ministry, and the weight of your responsibility in presenting Ellen Barrett and Annette Ruark for ordination to the priesthood. Therefore if any of you know any impediment or crime because of which we should not proceed, come forward now, and make it known.

Immediately, the Reverend James Wattley, the executive of a conservative group within the Church known as the Coalition for an Apostolic Ministry, came forward and read a statement saying that homosexuality was against Scripture. That was a most painful moment for Jim. I can think of no one who has more reverence for the service of ordination and for the Eucharist than he. He is a thorough Catholic brought up in a well-known clergy family, instilled with a deep respect for the Church and for its bishops. He and I have maintained a relationship of mutual respect. Jim had made an objection at an earlier woman's ordination as a representative of his committee. This time he made it clear that he spoke for himself alone. He read clearly, but his hands shook. Despite my disagreement with him I admired his moral courage. I thought to myself that he had done a tough thing well.

After the gospel, a professor from General Seminary preached the sermon and we proceeded with the ordination. As I placed my hands on Ellen's head, I had no doubts. I truly felt that this was right, according to what our Lord would have me do.

What priesthood needs most is integrity, love, and courage. These were Ellen's qualities. I trusted her. I knew that in the years to come she would represent Christ to hundreds of people and would serve Him unflinchingly. Annette, the other ordinand, was also a fine person, quiet and scholarly. It was hard for her to be caught up in this publicity, but she took it well and with good grace. At the end of the service they stood on either side of me, and as I put my hands on their shoulders, I said with tears in my eyes how proud I was, and what a fine moment this was in the life of the Church. The congregation applauded, the tension was released in a flood of affection as the Peace passed from one to another. A little girl sitting next to my wife said, "She is a girl like me, and she is a priest. Isn't that wonderful." The child then burst into tears.

Our procession led through the church door to the street, and chaos descended. Reporters, questions, shouts. "Bishop, you are wanted on the phone." "Bishop, come over here for a picture." "Bishop, wasn't it wonderful?" Meanwhile Ellen's press conference had begun inside the church. I thought to myself, "Holy Apostles Church will never be the same." An ex-convict who ran a prisoners' rehabilitation program at the church acted as a well-mannered bouncer when anyone started to get out of hand.

I had been through many crises both during the civil rights days and in the peace movement. I was used to criticism and knew that it was part of being a bishop. I had no idea, however, that the reaction to the ordination of a quiet young woman in a little downtown church would be more violent and last longer than all the rest of such experiences put together. The emotions in the civil rights crises came from the wells of racism. Those emotions in the peace movement sprang from patriotism mixed with the agony over fine young men giving up their lives in vain. But emotions arising from sexuality mixed with religion are even stronger and more volatile.

I have been asked whether I would have ordained Ellen had I known what the reaction would be. How can I tell? I might have waited awhile. If this had happened at a time when the Church was not already upset about the ordination of women, it might have caused less of a stir. If chance had sent along an admitted male homosexual, the emotions might have been less intense. When someone tells me how courageous it was to ordain Ellen I am inclined to say, "That's like saying it is courageous to be run over by a truck when you didn't see it coming."

I believe that if you go ahead with something after long thought and prayer and with the advice of others whom you respect, it will prove to have been the right thing. Or even if it causes harm, at least God will bring good out of it.

9

"With a bishop like you, small wonder there is so much rottenness, crime, and everything terrible in New York City"

The storm that followed the ordination of Ellen Barrett might have been too much for me, or at least my confidence might have been shaken, had it not been for a strange coincidence, a providential happening. Several months earlier I had accepted an invitation to spend an evening with the New York chapter of Integrity, the Episcopal Gay Fellowship. By chance it was the night after Ellen's ordination. Integrity meetings usually draw twenty or thirty people, gays and those sympathetic to them. They have an informal Eucharist, a discussion and coffee hour, very quiet and low key. I had accepted their invitation because I wanted to know them and to give them support. I also wanted to tell them my own views on their life in the Church. For instance, I felt strongly that a separate gay parish would be a mistake, and that their vocation was to fight for acceptance in their own parishes. At the same time, I felt that it was good for them to meet each week for mutual support, to make plans for the education of the Church on the issue of homosexuality, and to cooperate with other groups for gay rights legislation.

I arrived at the Integrity service a few minutes before eight P.M. The parish house was empty. I had a feeling that something was wrong, wrong time or wrong place. I checked my date book. I went to the door of the church and opened it. The cavernous old nave was full of people sitting quietly. The organ was playing. I must have made a mistake, I thought, it's probably a concert; that's the only thing that would draw a crowd like this on a Wednesday night. I went back to the sacristy. The rector rushed in: "Oh, there you are. We were beginning to worry."

"What's going on?" I asked. "That's a huge congregation in there."

"That congregation, my friend, is here for the Integrity Eucharist."

"Did you advertise in the *Village Voice* or on TV, or what? I was told that this was to be a low-key, off-the-record evening. I need publicity like a hole in the head right now!"

"Take it easy, Bishop," the rector said, patting me lightly on the shoulder. "We didn't advertise, the word just got around that you were going to be here, and that Ellen was probably going to be here, and the first thing we knew, the place was jammed. Relax and enjoy it. Everyone is really happy about the ordination."

Always one to take advice like relax and enjoy it, I did. What a beautiful experience it was, a church full of sympathetic people from all denominations. Even a rabbi was there. I preached about love and suffering, about how close they were to each other. I said that the true mark of the Church was being willing to suffer for love's sake, especially love for those who are cast out by society. I spoke about this particular congregation's familiarity with this kind of suffering, and how it had strengthened our Church on the deepest level. I concluded with the Resurrection, the new life which follows after redeemed pain. The future of the Church, I said, would be filled with new life when we were finally able to love everyone as he or she was made, as a child of God.

My theme was far from new, but I could feel it come alive in the faces looking up at me. In some way they had all experienced persecution because of their sexuality or their sympathy for homosexual persons. They knew what it was like to have to hide their love, their longings, their holiest feelings. They knew how it felt to be treated as less than human, as less than Christian, by the very Church of their beloved Saviour. They knew fear of the police, fear of being fired from their jobs, fear they might reach out and touch the wrong person and receive a blow instead of a smile. They understood the rejection of the Cross. I did not need to spell it out to them. But perhaps they had never heard their bishop speak to them in this way.

The Communion went on for what seemed a very long time. Many clergy were there. Everyone took his time in receiving, as if this were an especially holy interlude. I was moved by the expressions on their faces.

The coffee hour afterward was noisy, excited, and crowded. Person after person came up to thank me. I kept saying there was no need for thanks. Ellen would make a fine priest. I ordained her. No big deal. "Until now," one person said to me, "the Church has only offered to 'help' us. That is the very worst insult of all. We don't want that kind of condescending help. We don't want to be bundled off to a psychiatrist. Now someone in the Church, a bishop, our bishop, thank God, has ordained one of us. By doing that you stated that we are full human beings worthy of having a vocation to the highest calling of the Church. It's beautiful, man, it's beautiful!"

I saw old men with tortured expressions, faces that had had to mask their feelings for years. Older professional women, obviously successful in their careers. Young black men, a few servicemen, priests of our Church, Roman Catholic priests, including a member of the Jesuit order just refused ordination by his superiors because of his homosexuality; nuns, monks, businessmen; "hippies," three-piece suits, and blue jeans. Sensitive, aesthetic faces, fat faces, tough faces, bearded faces. Long hair, crew cuts. Orientals, Hispanics. Teenagers, grandmothers. And they came up to me as if I were a hero, some with tears in their eyes. I was embraced by perfect strangers as if I were a long-cherished friend. It was one of the most loving, accepting, heart-warming experiences I have ever had. I left with one remark resounding in my mind: "Now we can walk as Christians with our heads held high."

During the difficult times ahead I remembered that night. When I was under pressure from so many people and I began to wonder if I had done the right thing, I remembered that remark. When I thought that perhaps I had let down the morality of the Church as so many said, I remembered those faces receiving Communion and filled with love for their Lord. When I was told I had hurt the feelings of righteous Episcopalians, I thought of the faces hurt by years of prejudice and anger, and how even those faces had been filled, that night, with joy. If I was wrong, then at least the Lord brought something good out of it for so many of His people.

I drove home from the Integrity meeting full of hope that night. As Brenda and I settled in for a nightcap, I shuffled through the day's mail. My euphoria was brief. The mail was full of letters from my brother bishops and others who were upset.

The Church is a political institution. Bishops, who are elected by the Church and who serve as its chief administrative officers, are, among other things, political persons. I do not use the word "political" as an insult. I have always resented the juxtaposition of the words "politician" and "statesman." You are a politician if you do something and are reelected. You are a statesman if you do something and are not reelected. One tends to characterize bishops in somewhat the same way. If you do things your people agree with, and raise a lot of money, you are just an administrator. If you raise hell and get people upset, some call you a prophet,

others call you a heretic. The thing that really bothered my
brother bishops the most, I think, was the trouble Ellen Barrett's ordination was causing them in their own dioceses. A
bishop can splash around as much as he likes in his own
pond so long as it does not make waves beyond his shores.
But when something happens like the illegal ordination of
women in Philadelphia, which gets into the media and stirs
up every parish church in the country, then the bishops rear
up and take off after the culprits.

My misjudgment was that Ellen's ordination at most would
make a splash only in my own diocese, one more crazy thing
happening in New York. But at that time in history, most
of the country was watching with some satisfaction the proud
Empire City going bankrupt, and most of the Church was
still fascinated by the idea of women priests. The news of
the ordination was published in every little paper in the country. It was a human-interest story no self-respecting city editor
could pass up, sex and religion all tied up in a titillating
little story with a New York dateline.

Here is a letter to me from the South, in response to that
news:

Sir: I am so disgusted with you (believe me, the Holy Apostles
must be turning in their graves) and the whole city of New York.
How you could ever ordain such a filthy rotten creature? If I had
the money I would get to New York and stop that horrible ceremony. With a bishop like you, small wonder there is so much rotten-
ness, crime and everything terrible in your city. God killed everyone
in Sodom and Gomorrah, and it is high time that a tidal wave
should wash away New York City.
You positively make me regurgitate.

And a letter from Pennsylvania:

. . . It grieves me to be so bold as to admonish a Bishop, elevated
to that high office in Christ's Church by the devout people of the

Episcopal persuasion, on matters pertaining to the spiritual health
of the whole Body of Christ. I pray for those in high authority to
give Christ-like leadership to their respective churches.

As the evening paper revealed "Lesbian Priest" with a byline
"Episcopal Bishop Ordains Ellen Barrett," I wept as if another
spike was driven through our blessed Lord Jesus. . . .

My fellow bishops began to receive letters like these, and
phone calls, and resolutions from their parishes. Most were
already feeling besieged because of the ordination of women
and the new Prayer Book, which contained radical changes
in familiar services and altered many beloved words. We had
all gone home from the Minneapolis General Convention
intending to calm things down and keep the Church together.
Then Ellen Barrett. All hell broke loose. Bishops could not
defend the action, and yet it was done within the canon law.
For parishes which they were barely able to keep in the
Church before, this was the "last straw" and a reason to
leave. Wealthy contributors cut their pledges. It is no wonder
that I received so many angry letters from my colleagues. I
must also add that most of them genuinely disagreed with
what I did. However, I believe pressures from within their
own dioceses were responsible, to a large extent, for their
angry feelings.

The morning after the Integrity service I knew that we
were in a crisis. To decide how to handle it, I met with my
suffragan bishops, Stuart Wetmore and the late Harold
Wright, whose judgment and candor I trust absolutely. We
knew that the usual polite answers to letters would not be
enough, and so we co-opted one of our most able lay staff
persons to help answer the mail. We also decided that I
should send out a statement to all the bishops of the Church
and to all the clergy of my diocese. This meant a mailing
of about seven hundred pieces. Furthermore, if the unrest
in the diocese did not subside, perhaps some regional meet-

ings would be in order. Bishop Wetmore was not so sure about that idea, so we put it aside for the time being.

The statement to the bishops and clergy was not easy to write. It had to be clear and absolutely factual. It needed a theological rationale and wording that would be sensitive to both the homosexual community and to those who were upset by the ordination. I did not want to sound defensive or arrogant. I wanted to sound confident but not cocksure about what I had done. I consulted Canon Walter Dennis at our cathedral, who has been a scholar in the field of religion and human sexuality for many years; and I consulted two of the faculty at General Seminary to make sure that I did not commit any theological gaffes. When it was written, I read it to Ellen Barrett to be sure it did not offend her. It was mailed on January 18, 1977, eight days after the ordination. A covering letter went to the bishops as follows:

Dear Brothers:

I have heard from several of you concerning the much-publicized ordination of Ellen Marie Barrett. For this reason a mailing to the whole House seemed indicated.

I enclose a statement which contains some material I hope you will find useful. May I underline some salient points:

1. Ellen Barrett was ordained legally with the firm consent of the Standing Committee which represents a cross section of our Diocese.
2. We in no way looked on this as a "first" or an unusual event. Rather, she was chosen as a whole person worthy (if any of us is) of ordination by our full canonical process, by those persons designated by the Church to make such decisions.
3. Ellen is a quiet, rather reserved person of academic interests. She is no militant nor one who would wish to impose her views on others.
4. Persons known, or virtually known, to be homosexual have been ordained for years. The only difference between such persons, whom many of us have ordained, and Ellen Barrett is her candor. Candor, or, if you will, honesty is not a bar to ordination.

5. We were all dismayed by the publicity. I regret if it has caused you so much difficulty, and I hope this letter and the enclosure at least explains "where we are coming from."

Best wishes for the New Year.

STATEMENT

On Monday, December 15, 1975, I ordained Ellen Marie Barrett a Deacon, and on Monday, January 10, 1977, I ordained her a Priest. I acted in full knowledge of her professed homosexual orientation, believing (as I still do) that she was fully qualified in every way for holy orders.

Ellen first applied to me informally in 1972. At that time she was fairly active in the Gay Movement and had written an article or two on the subject. I told her then that I would not recommend her to the Standing Committee. She later applied to the Diocese of Pennsylvania, but was not accepted there. She was serious about her vocation, however, and matriculated at The General Theological Seminary. Early in 1975 she reapplied for candidacy in the Diocese of New York. She had by then resigned her office in "Integrity" and ceased to be active in the Gay Movement. More important, I was convinced that her vocation to ordination had deepened; she professed this vocation to ministry, service, and teaching as her consuming interest. Her recommendation from The General Theological Seminary was excellent in terms of character, personality, behavior and academic competence.

Ellen went through the rigorous screening process of the Diocese of New York, which includes a weekend conference with the Ministries Commission. She also passed the canonically required psychiatric examination which is designed to screen out those emotionally unfit for the ministry. (It is worth noting in this context that the American Psychiatric Association, the professional organization of psychiatrists, has declared that homosexuality as such is not an illness.)

I presented her to the Standing Committee, and she was admitted as a candidate on May 8, 1975. She was approved for the Diaconate on November sixth of that year. The news of Ellen's impending ordination to the Diaconate was picked up by an unfriendly source, and news releases were sent throughout the country. As a result we had several letters objecting to her ordination. I called a special meeting of the Standing Committee, which unanimously reaffirmed its approval of her ordination to the Diaconate.

The fact that she had publicly admitted her homosexual orientation was not judged by the Bishop or the Standing Committee to be a barrier to ordination. All of us were aware that many homosexual persons have been ordained into the ministry of the Church over the years and have served the Church well. They were, of course, forced to be very secretive about this aspect of their personality. Now it is possible to be more open about one's sexual orientation, and that is a healthy development.

The personal morality, lifestyle, and behavior of every ordinand must be and is carefully weighed by the Bishop, the Ministries Commission, and the Standing Committee. This applies to persons of all sexual orientations. In the absence of public scandal, however, the personal morality of an ordinand becomes almost by definition a matter between him or her and a confessor, pastor or bishop. Suffice it to say that Ellen Barrett's life and profession had not been an occasion of public scandal.

In approving persons for ordination, the Bishop, Standing Committee, and Ministries Commission deal with each person as a whole and as an individual. It is an intensely personal judgment and does not lend itself to categories. Ellen Barrett, judged as a whole person, was determined by us to possess a valid vocation to the diaconate and priesthood, and to have the character and competence to fulfill this vocation. Her ordination was not a political act and did not seek to make a statement about homosexual activity; it was, like any ordination, the solemn laying on of hands upon a person carefully and prayerfully chosen.

Prejudices passed down through the centuries have made it difficult for most of us to make a genuinely Christian judgment of the homosexual condition. We know, however, that a great deepening and broadening of our understanding of human sexuality has emerged in recent years, nurtured by the interaction between traditional Christian theology and our modern world's perception of human nature. There has, for one thing, been decided movement in the Church away from a tradition which grudgingly accepted sex for procreative ends only toward a more encompassing, psychosomatic view of sexuality as a good and desirable way of expressing a loving relationship between persons. One telling result of this theological shift is the general acceptance within the Anglican communion of birth control as a fully moral practice.

In shifting away from an exclusively procreative view of sex to one of sex as a human expression of love, we move beyond explicit Biblical guidance. I pray that the Holy Spirit will guide us. The Church has reawakened to the realization that Truth is an open-ended process of progressive revelation, and what we are witnessing in our time with regard to human sexuality is just such a process.

For most people, however, this rethinking of the morality of sexual expression is yet to be extended to homosexual persons.

I believe that their recognition as full members of the Church with the opportunities, rights, and responsibilities of all other members is based ultimately on Jesus' view of human nature as reflected in the Gospel. Again and again, He broke through the prejudices of the day to accept and lift up those rejected and downgraded by others. And just as the reasons for their rejection were often beyond their control, so the homosexual person's condition is generally not a matter of conscious choice.

The forces that shape sexual orientation are still somewhat mysterious, but there is general agreement that our sexuality is forged at an incredibly early age, long before puberty. Thus, a person's sexual preference is not in the category of sin, and the sometimes violent social prejudice against the homosexual condition comes painfully close to the recorded targets of Jesus' preaching.

As a Church, we are only beginning to work out the complicated issues in the area of human sexuality. I plan to have some conferences in the near future to help us all in our thinking. Meanwhile, for those of you who have an interest in exploring the issue of the moment, I have listed some books that might prove helpful.

The Same Sex. Ralph Weltge, ed. Pilgrim Press, 1969
Time for Consent. N. Pittenger. SCM Press, 1967
The Church and the Homosexual. John J. McNeill, S. J. Sheed, Andrews and McNeill, 1976

The Bishop of Long Island is an old and dear friend. He is highly respected by his brother bishops, and for several years was the vice chairman of the House of Bishops. Jonathan Sherman is a man of total integrity, pastoral concern, and scholarly intellect. His churchmanship is Catholic in orientation but flexible. He is open-minded. My differences with him would be the differences of a younger with an older man, one who has been exposed a little more than he to some of the currents of the younger generation in a city of *avant garde* thinking. Jon sent a mailing to his clergy the same day I sent out my statement. It mentioned the inhibition of one of his clergy for canonical behavior and included a copy of a telegram to another of his priests who had come out in favor of starting a schismatic church because of the ordination of women, and a copy of a letter to me concerning the ordination of Ellen Barrett. My neighboring bishop has many problems. I was sorry to add to them.

His letter outlined a theory of the psychodynamics of homosexuality as an arresting of a person's development on the homosexual level. He distinguished among various kinds of homosexuals: those retarded sexually, those with a responsible commitment to another, and those who are promiscuous and exploitative. Ordination of a homosexual person, he wrote, would make a priest of someone who was not a "wholesome example," and would confuse the members of the Church and the general public with regard to the three types of homosexuals he had distinguished.

Although I am sure that most of his people would have agreed with his conclusion, I received a copy of a letter to him from a clinical psychologist in his diocese who took him to task for his psychological statements. He wrote:

> While it is true that the mental health community is not in agreement on the causes and meaning of homosexuality, and true that your position (as far as I can understand it from your letter) is one which used to be held by some mental health professionals, a more thorough knowledge of the field would have made it apparent that professionals now tend to see sexual orientation as a "given" of the human situation. Homosexual orientation is, therefore, as much a fact of the human condition as heterosexual orientation is.
>
> Support for this view, readily available had you chosen to consult it, comes from clinical evidence from professionals who work with homosexual persons. If homosexuality were a matter of some defect in maturation, we would expect that some form of clinical intervention would help to cure it, as such interventions do with so many other forms of emotional immaturity or delayed emotional development. The clinical literature clearly shows, however, that *no* form of intervention, from psychoanalysis to the techniques of behavior modification, has had *any* success in producing long-term (let alone permanent) change in any person's sexual orientation. Of course, this does not include those persons for whom their homosexuality is used as a defense against even more primitive and unacceptable impulses (but even here the success rate is very low), although one assumes that your letter was not directed toward such persons.
>
> As your view of homosexuality is so far removed from the best

of current thinking, I surely cannot be the only doctor in the Diocese who is embarrassed to see such a potentially destructive opinion put forth by the Bishop.

This has been one of the difficulties throughout the whole debate. No one can agree on the psychological or medical facts of homosexuality. And on these facts, of course, theological and moral judgments had to be based.

Another bishop threw discretion to the winds and wrote, "Isn't it time we called things by their right names, not deviant behavior but sin, not a call girl but a whore or prostitute, not a playboy but a whore monger, not a gay but a homosexual." He went on:

We are all lumped together. I shall be sharing the priesthood with a lesbian. Is this fair? I know I am a sinner and have plenty to account for, but I have never tried to make a virtue of sin. This falsifying of the truth is the worst aspect of the whole thing. This was the kind of doctrine on which Hitler thrived.

Other groups in the Church that have problems with the ordination are the evangelicals and the charismatics. Loosely defined, an evangelical is one who emphasizes Jesus's life and teaching and tends to take Scripture literally. The charismatics believe in the "baptism of the Spirit," an emotional conversion experience leading to a very fervent spiritual life, including speaking in tongues and an almost fundamentalist view of Scripture. It is difficult for both these groups to understand the concept of the evolving revelation of God's word, even though Jesus Himself said that His disciples could not bear to hear all the truth at one time and that the Holy Spirit would continue to reveal the truth to them. John 14:25: "These things have I spoken to you while I am still with you. But the Counselor, the Holy Spirit, whom the Father will send in my name, he will teach you all things and bring to remembrance all that I have said to you." Thus, because homosexuality is condemned by St. Paul in the New Testament, they reject the possibility that a deeper understanding of that nature than existed in St. Paul's time might change the traditional attitude into one of loving acceptance toward persons who, through no fault of their own, are so constituted. Several of our bishops are of this charismatic or evangelical persuasion. I received a letter from one of these bishops, who summed up his views in the last paragraph of his letter:

> I love you as a brother in Christ, but I will do everything I can to see that this kind of behavior is stopped, for I believe it represents theological distortion that will have an increasingly devastating effect on the struggles people have to maintain [for] a sense of personal integrity, family unity, social well-being and loyalty to Christ.

I was not particularly upset by this bishop's letter, which was courteous, but I was a little irritated that many parishes in his diocese were conducting what amounted to a vendetta on the subject. I received many resolutions and several hundred letters from his diocese. Oddly enough, many of them were in the same hand, and others had the same wording. However, some laymen in that diocese were equally irritated by the mail campaign. One wrote to his bishop:

> . . . Because of this controversy I have received copies of various letters and resolutions, including your letter of January 25, 1977 to Bishop Moore. I just have to tell you very frankly that I am appalled that churches have nothing better to do than to spend their energies on criticism of the actions of one bishop. I haven't counted them, but I would estimate that there are many more than 100 dioceses in the Episcopal Church. Bishop Moore, then, represents less than one percent of all the bishops. As far as I can determine, the action of the three parishes which passed resolutions condemning Bishop Moore was taken without any attempt to have him explain and justify his action. This seems to me to be strange conduct for priests and lay leaders.

Many bishops dealt with the issue in addresses to their own conventions. One bishop said, in part:

In facing the winds of change that blow just now, I wish we might prevail to alter the course of two. They seem ill winds to me. I speak of the erosion of commitment to life-long marriage, and the steady drift toward a sanction of homosexuality as an in-born given, like skin color or physical height. I do not abandon the old norms that have girded our resolve and guided our growing up into mature manhood and womanhood. Marriage and sexuality are incendiary issues. They are banked and bursting fires, made so by the immense human energy given us by God in giving us our sexuality. But human energy by the highest norms is by defini-tion *out of control.* It is bound to be destructive, personally and socially.

Here is our problem as the Church: How may we hold fast to monog-amous life-long marriage as the God-given norm in a healthy society and yet reach out in understanding and strength for those who suffer breaking and broken marriages? How to regard homosexual-ity as an amenable personality disorder, which is how I view it, and yet insist upon a true and loving regard for persons?

Though I personally esteem the Rt. Rev. Paul Moore, Jr., I would not answer this painful difficulty as he and the Diocese of New York have sought to deal with it. The Church's long tradition and my own convictions, formed through two years of reading, reflect-ing and much dialogue, forbid my ordaining an avowed homosex-ual—though a vestry, the Standing Committee and the Commission on Ministry might authorize me to do so—which had to be the case in New York according to our canon law. No bishop may ordain anyone apart from a process of exhaustive examination and representative consent. There are no easy answers; only the cer-tainty that we are called to stand with one another in suffering— and that God will light our way and heal us, or sustain us in our brokenness with the gift of endurance as we open our lives to his holiness.

Although most of the members of the House of Bishops are men who have come up through the ranks as parish priests, there are a few who have been elected from the Church's seminaries. They are professional theologians and tend to have more than their share of influence in the House discussions. Bishop Arthur Vogel of the Diocese of West Missouri is one. I find his theologizing needlessly complex and convoluted. His views are more conservative than mine, and he has spent his ministry in other parts of the country, which is good reason for us to differ.

My tendency is to look at the gospel immersed in the world, and to see it as the salvation for the persons caught in suffering and confusion. Thus I feel that the love and compassion of God as revealed in Jesus is the overriding message by which all other theological niceties and traditions must be judged. If something keeps someone from the love of God, it is wrong. This is my understanding of why St. Paul, for example, insisted that circumcision not be required of the Gentiles who wanted to become Christians. Bishop Vogel, on the other hand, seems to see the world from within the Church, and tends in his theology to protect the Church and to reject persons or ideas which might interfere with its purity and therefore its power. Also he is most concerned that we do nothing to jeopardize our relations with the Roman Catholic Church, with whom he has been one of our most active liaisons. The following excerpt is from an article he wrote for his diocesan paper in January 1977.

Since the bishop of each diocese, by his sacramental office, presents and represents the universal church to the people of his local diocese, as a brother in Christ, I must report the deeply deleterious effects of Ms. Barrett's ordination upon the clergy and people of this diocese. Shock wave after shock wave of disappointment and bewilderment are striking the faithful in this portion of God's vineyard. . . .

The difficulty in which we now find ourselves once again involves the nature of episcopacy and the relationship of individual bishops to the wider, universal church. Bishops, as individuals, may not appropriate their sacramental functions to their personal views. The demand to accept a controverted life style, for example, in the name of the sacramental recognition of Holy Orders is to misuse and appropriate a communal expression to one's own perspective. It is to make a sacrament a means to an end extrinsic to its nature. So to use a sacrament as a means to an end beyond itself in an argument is to damage the sacrament's effectiveness in the very community it is supposed to serve. The subversion of the church's sacramental structure to the opinions and positions of individuals is what the church must not allow!

In advocating different positions within the church, partisans should argue in such a way that they alone bear the consequences of their argument. That is where Christian charity has failed us in recent years.

As usual, there were stout defenders on the other side ready to reply:

Dear Bishop Vogel:

I read with interest your comments in the January Diocesan Bulletin touching on the ordination by Bishop Moore of Ms. Barrett. . . .

Surely you must also know that bishops (some of them gay themselves) have been ordaining gay priests for generations (though, unlike the honest Bishop Moore, saying nothing about it). If the gay priests of the Church were all required to leave the ministry, you would be hard put to it to get marginal coverage for the cures now in many cases ably served by hard-working, godly, and effective priests. You may never know which of your clergy are homosexual (and, by the way, most of them are married and have children). And now that you have declared yourself so openly hostile to these people, you may be sure that those who might have been open with you about it will be most careful to keep the fact from you. . . .

One senses that you have neglected to consider the evidence of the fruit of Bishop Moore's ministry, a witness pretty nearly without equal in the Episcopal Church. Does not that ministry of his over the past years commend to you the wisdom of some trust both of his judgment and his motivation in this ordination?

The Southern dioceses comprise another political grouping within the House of Bishops. As in the U.S. Senate, they tend to have more influence than the strength of their dioceses warrants. Traditionally the South has consecrated its bishops at a fairly young age, thus giving them seniority as they stay on in the House over the years. They tend to be a solid political unit. They have deep friendships with one another, usually have attended the same seminaries, meet together frequently, and come out of the same cultural, political, and theological background. Their posture tends to be conservative (I do not use the term pejoratively), and evangelical, and rests on the Church's upholding the traditional morality of the community. With the election of the Bishop of Mississippi as Presiding Bishop, their influence has grown stronger, even though they are no longer as homogeneous as they once were. The following letter is from one of them:

I am sure you have heard from almost everybody concerning the ordination of Ellen Marie Barrett. By now you must realize how very much harm has been done to our Church by your action.

I have read your written defense of your action with great interest. I agree with much of it in principle. However, I think you made three errors so serious that they can only be considered sinful:

(1) The timing of this ordination was almost certain to cause it to be confused with the issue of ordination of women. . . .

(2) I think it was incredibly naïve for you to think that this ordination would not receive widespread publicity at this time. . . .

(3) When you *were* questioned by the news media about the ordination, apparently you did not at any point make clear that you were not approving homosexual *practices* or *acts*. *Time* magazine apparently quotes Ms. Barrett as saying that the strength of her ministry comes from her relationship with her lesbian lover. If she has been incorrectly quoted, and is not a *practicing* homosexual, then I assume she has entered suit against *Time* magazine, and that you have joined her in that suit. If not, I think both of you have a duty to do so.

Paul, I feel very angry and very much betrayed by this action on your part. I took leadership in the House of Bishops to help the House lean so far over backwards in dealing with the Philadelphia Eleven and the Washington Four that I thought we deserved better than this. The next day you gave very emotional expression to your gratitude towards me and others in the House. In view of that, I find it impossible to understand your recent action which causes embarrassment and confusion and harm to all of us, and to the Church we seek to serve.

I was beginning to be angry myself. The argument was heating up. It seems the bishops were more disturbed by the publicity than the substance. I answered:

I am sorry that my action has caused you difficulty, and it's hard to have to opt for either stupidity or sinfulness. I'll let you be the judge of which I am guilty. I did make clear to the media time and again that I was not approving homosexual acts and I also have that on my written statement which you received several weeks ago. Ellen Barrett, I found out after that statement, was misquoted in *Time*. She never said what she is quoted as saying. In fact, she has never spoken about her personal life with any of the media. I did ask a lawyer about bringing suit, but apparently it's practically an impossible thing to do.

Finally, I don't see why you associate the Philadelphia Eleven and the Washington Four with the ordination of Ellen Barrett. I don't feel that we store up little favors for one another in the House of Bishops, but, rather, that we do what we feel we must in good conscience, and act for the good of the Church as far as we can determine it. I still meant my expression of gratitude for you and others in the House and will continue to mean it, but I don't see why this should be a barrier to the Standing Committee and I ordaining someone whom we felt qualified for the priesthood whose only difference with literally hundreds of others of our clergy was her candor.

It should not appear that none of the bishops was sympathetic. I did receive phone calls and notes of encouragement from a few bishops, and many of those critical of the action were friendly and sympathetic to me personally. But I also had a few surprises. For example, my correspondence with a brilliant, socially concerned liberal of the forties and fifties, to whom I wrote after he published a critical column in the newspaper:

. . . There are literally thousands of people who because of their homosexual orientation suffer persecution—both overt and by implication. They were deeply touched and strengthened by the symbolic aspect of this ordination. We did not think of it as a test case in any way, yet when it was lifted up as such it revitalized a great many people even though it also upset others.

I feel that I have maintained the faith and defended the spirit of the Gospel. You are free to disagree, of course.

And his response:

I am convinced that never, never, never must that ordination be a precedent, that the life of the Church is at stake, that nothing in all my ministry has troubled me more or shaken my confidence in the Episcopal Church as much, that it has been fantastically divisive, that it has taken our eyes off the main task of the Church, and that I will continue to pray that you will acknowledge it to have been a grave mistake. It would be good for the Church, and for you also, if you could do this.

I agree with you that the civil rights of homosexuals must be respected and defended; but that does not mean we ordain practicing homosexuals and thereby morally approve of homosexuality and throw a question mark around the whole ministry. If your action ever became a precedent, I would be compelled to make a most difficult decision.

I would predict—wishing you well—that if you do not make clear this action of yours is no precedent, this matter will tumble and undermine your whole episcopate. It already has.

It was hard for me to understand how one who had had so much insight and courage on earlier issues could be so blind on this one. His pain is apparent in the letter. Oddly enough, his successor sent me the following:

I think your statement on the homosexual issue was superb. It is hard for me to realize how anyone with good sense and Christian love could take issue with your reasoning, which is set forth so well. Keep in there. You have my support.

Bob DeWitt, who knew Ellen, wrote this supportive letter:

I noted the fact of the recent ordination of Ellen Barrett to the priesthood, and want to commend you for your role in having made that possible.

I have known Ellen for many years, have worked with her and have had an opportunity to observe her work. She is a person of eminent qualifications for priesthood, and I rejoice in the fact of her ordination.

Since many people have taken exception to that ordination without the benefit of knowing Ellen, I wanted to let you know that, based upon my knowing her very well, I could not be more enthusiastic.

Others followed:

Please don't forget, good friend, that there are legions of us who support you in your decisions about ordinations these days, despite the fact that we don't rush into print to tell you so. But it's a fact.

Hang in there. We're rooting for you.

I am not given to writing fan letters but now that I am reading material critical of your action in ordaining a lesbian, I cannot keep silent and want you to know how much I admire you for what you did and the "intestinal fortitude" which enabled you to do it! Not only do I entirely agree that some of our best priests are homosexual but in no way do I find homosexual orientation a bar to an effective ministry. My mind goes back—long before you were a bishop—when we were discussing this subject in the House and Ben Washburn rose to say that he wouldn't change one of his homosexual clergy for six "normal" ones. Indeed when I was a member of the Committee on Pastoral Counseling I proposed that we take a stand to the effect that we believe homosexuality to be no more of a sin than it ought to be a crime—but no one would support me and even Mollegen from Virginia Theological School could come up with nothing better than celibacy!

I know, Paul, that you are the sort who is able to fight his own battles, but I also wanted you to know that from this side there are those cheering you on!

From one of the bishops who ordained the first women, illegally, in Philadelphia:

As one who is not unacquainted with flak, I am feeling for you these days and identifying with you. I've been daily praying for you by name since July 29, 1974, but in recent weeks I've been praying quite a bit more earnestly.

I tell you what I tell myself: If your informed conscience bids you do it, don't let *anyone* bluff you or pressure you out of going forward. The only judge who matters ultimately is God.

I rejoice in your courage and firm faith, Paul. You give fresh heart to many.

These last three were from bishops brought up in the Northeast. Cultural background does affect one's understanding of the gospel, I am convinced. This, I think, was at the very heart of the controversy. While no one can have an absolute fix on the gospel, because it is too universal and too sweeping in its comprehension, can we not, however, respect each other's actions and interpretations?

Perhaps the most thoughtful, clear, and supportive document in those early weeks was written by a retired bishop who had taught in seminary, been a parish priest, and fought an ugly civil rights battle in his own diocese.

The high degree of irrationality existing in human institutions generally and in the Episcopal Church in particular has been vividly shown in the furor aroused by the ordination of Ellen Barrett to the priesthood. Great pressure has been put upon diocesan bishops to disavow and condemn the act. The straightforward statement of the Bishop of New York, giving reasons for his action, has been largely ignored. Shock, hurt, fear, anger, in one instance the ridiculous flying of the Church flag upside down on a parish flag pole, all have given the impression that the very foundations of Christian faith and morality have been threatened by the ordination of one woman, honest enough to admit her lesbian tendencies.

Several attitudes and assumptions seem especially unfortunate:

1. Many people have assumed a knowledge about homosexuality unwarranted by the facts available. No one really knows a great deal about the subject, about its causes, the possibility or even the desirability of its cure or the reasons for the taboo against it in many, but by no means all human cultures. We do know that in any society there are a considerable number of homosexuals and many more people quite capable of homosexual as well as heterosexual relationships. Only very recently has anyone tried to compile statistics or make estimates of the numbers and percentages involved. We know even less about past societies. It is well indeed for the Church to study human sexuality in depth, although one questions whether or not we have the means or the capacity to do so fairly and objectively. In the meantime, it is foolish to quote Biblical texts that reflect far different cultural conditions in a manner that suggests a literalist or pre-critical attitude toward the interpretation of scripture or a naïve natural theology that takes little account of actual biological and psychological complexities.

2. Many people seem to assume that until more is known about homosexuality, homosexuals should not be ordained. However, it will be a long time before Christians agree on this sensitive subject, judging by the emotional level of the current comments. In the meantime, shall we deny that homosexual persons can be called to the priesthood or demand from them a standard of celibacy not expected of others? One bishop writes, "I am convinced that they [homosexual patterns of behavior] fall far short of the true meaning of sexuality although they are not necessarily devoid of value and dignity."

Most patterns of behavior fall far short of the true meaning, not only of sexuality, but of God's purpose for our entire lives. Can anything more be expected of Christians, ordained or un-ordained, than they strive to live lives of value and dignity, always knowing how short we fall and how great is our need of for-giveness? Can anyone say with assurance that God's purpose for the homosexual is something other than living out his nature with dignity?

3. It is very distressing to note that some people are willing for homosexuals to be ordained, as indeed a great many of them always have been, provided they do not admit their inclinations publicly. Thus we shall perpetuate a conspiracy of silence with its guilt, fear and hypocrisy. Critics seem to have overlooked the fact that many homosexuals feel called to minister to the "gay" community, to people seeking to find and maintain a human and Christian identity. Can this be done from the closet or with the tacit assumption that such folk must "repent" by denying them-selves to a degree not required of others?

I am not much impressed by arguments about not offending against the scruples and consciences of fellow Christians. Paul's admonitions in this regard dealt only with refraining from eating meat offered to idols, no great sacrifice for anyone. But Christians must learn to live with fellow Christians who are homosexual, just as Jewish Christians had to learn to live with Gentile converts. Bitter trauma seems to have been or to be involved in both instances.

Obviously, certain kinds of publicity are in bad taste, although in the case of the recent ordination the publicity seems largely to have been the result of the protests against it. Publicity was probably inevitable in this instance; to cite it as a reason for cancell-ing the ordination is indeed unfair and unjust.

4. Once again the doctrine of "collegiality" in the House of Bishops is advanced as an argument for inaction or delay. Obviously bishops should consult and counsel with each other on matters of substantial consequence to the faith and to the Church, but for them to *bind* themselves and each other to certain courses of action is to circumvent the constitutional and canonical procedures provided for the orderly governing of the Church as well as to abdicate the responsibility for leadership laid upon bishops by the very virtue of their office. There may be extreme instances when certain bishops—alone or with others—feel that they must go be-yond normal canonical rules, but to interpose a binding of collegial-ity is to exceed constitutional standards.

5. The protests show little or no evidence of dialogue with homo-sexual persons or communities, of listening to their needs, aspira-

tions and anxieties, to how they understand and value their sexuality and relate it to the whole of their Christian profession. This brings to mind similar insensitivities such as white people discussing among themselves (often very charitably) how far to go in granting freedom or civil rights to Black people, or men deciding among themselves whether women should have the right to vote or be ordained as priests.

6. Finally, this episode demonstrates the need for much more study of taboos. In the Book of Leviticus the taboo against homosexuality is listed among many others having to do with diet and conduct. Some, if not all, such taboos may have been necessary for the preservation of the distinctive character of the people of God, even for their survival in a time of small populations and many hazards to their health and identity. The taboo against homosexuality may even have something permanent to say about the organization of society and the role of male and female.

Much more urgent, however, is the need for developing other taboos necessary for human survival in our day. We need taboos against waste and pollution of human resources that could rob our children of life and health, taboos perhaps against several cars for at least most families, against overpopulation and the alleged right of every couple on earth to have as many children as they wish; taboos against development of nuclear energy, a far greater threat to the human race than almost any number of homosexuals. And need we not develop taboos against violence and the attitude that one man shooting another or beating him into unconsciousness is somehow natural while two people embracing in love, whatever their sex, is not?

Are there not more consequential areas in which to expend our energies and to seek to learn the will of God for our time?

The bishops wrote to me from personal, theological, and political concerns; and they wrote from pastoral concern that their people had been hurt and confused by my action. But I have never felt that it was the responsibility of a pastor to protect his people from the confusion which comes to them from the world and the Church, but rather to give them strength and wisdom and compassion to deal with that confusion. Compared to the hurt and confusion of homosexual Christians over the years, the quandary of a few insecure and respectable people seems minor.

Among all the bishops who wrote to me in those first three

months, I received ten positive letters and thirty-two negative ones. When we met at the annual House of Bishops in the fall of 1977, three-to-one against were approximately the odds I encountered there as well.

10

"... Their kingdom was small and full of uproar."
II Esdras 12:2

Once there is publicity around an event, the clear-cut lines begin to blur. Issues other than the main one become the focus. You fulminate at the media, scream about reporters, become paranoid, think that "they" are out to get you, that "they" will do anything for a story. So has it always been. Long before television or even modern times, local village gossip worked the same way. It is simply a fact of life and you deal with it as best you can. The letters and other communications which follow reveal the enormous variety of feelings with which people of conscience reacted to this rather small event.

One morning in February 1977, I was sitting in the kitchen of a Lutheran pastor in Philadelphia, in whose church I had preached the night before. The news was on the radio: "The Presiding Bishop of the Episcopal Church accuses Bishop Moore of New York of breaking an agreement . . ." The New York *Post* that day carried the same story, datelined Richmond, Va., and headed "Lesbian Priest: More Flak":

The presiding bishop of the 2.7 million member Episcopal Church says Episcopal Bishop Paul Moore of New York didn't use good judgment when he ordained an acknowledged lesbian.

130

[Bishop John] Allin told a press conference here that he has received "one or two" formal requests to force Moore to resign. But he said he has no power to do anything to a diocesan bishop.

Allin said there was a "general understanding" among bishops before the Barrett ordination that no one would knowingly ordain a homosexual before the Church could study the matter of sexuality.

I fumed and spluttered over my eggs. My host was duly sympathetic. He said they did not have presiding bishops in the Lutheran Church. I said that maybe I should be a Lutheran. On the way up to New York on the train, I scrawled a hot note to the Presiding Bishop, and felt a little better by the time we passed the cheerful landscape of Perth Amboy:

I had been about to write you and thank you for your neutrality on the Barrett ordination; that you had decided not to stand in judgment of a fellow bishop, and then came the shock of the enclosed release. I trust it is inaccurate.

I know of no understanding among bishops about the ordination of those of homosexual orientation; neither does Stuart Wetmore. Where or when was such an understanding agreed upon?

I hope you realize how this pulls the rug out from under me in a very difficult and delicate situation. I held fast on women's ordination before Minneapolis because of our House of Bishops' agreement. I do not break promises, Jack. I feel you have impugned my integrity.

Although it is purely personal, Brenda and I were particularly upset that this occurred in her home town where her parents still live.

I trust you will retract this statement.

Before mailing it, I checked with Bishop Wetmore and Bishop Wright to make sure my memory was accurate. Stuart Wetmore has a memory which makes the average elephant look like an absent-minded professor, and he remembered no such agreement. Nor did Bishop Wright. Jack Allin responded as follows:

In response to your confidential letter I regret any unnecessary distress you may be experiencing. It has not been my intention to add to your problems in any way. I have not accused you of breaking any promises.

News reports which provide half truths and half statements are as distressing to me as to you. They do seem inevitable in our society, since the news media is not only a source of pressure but is under pressure. Controversial issues become increasingly complicated by the news media's effort to report.

You know, I am sure, that I too have been plagued with requests for news interviews concerning the Barrett ordination. Here in the office I have been able to regulate the interview requests. During visits throughout the country, however, the matter is more difficult and the best response is made infrequently or lost in the shuffle of the news conference.

Richmond was a classic case. Questions concerning the Barrett ordination were the first asked. In responding I attempted to give as accurate and balanced answers as possible. Less than half of my response was reported.

Note that "general understanding" is in quotation marks. My statement to the press in Richmond was that many of the bishops felt there was a "general understanding" that no homosexual would be ordained, at least until after the study of the subject as called for by the General Convention when some new understanding might be reached. I pointed out that some of the bishops had complained that you had not waited for the results of that study. I did not say you had broken an agreement. To my knowledge you did not enter an agreement. No formal agreement was stated or voted upon in the House that I remember.

In that interview I also stated that in my opinion you are an "idealist," adding that idealists are often accused of unrealistic decisions. I attempted to point out that in reaching your decision regarding the ordination in question, you were not attempting to make a test case.

As you know, correcting impressions received from press reports is a near impossible task. I can say this with some emphasis, having been a subject of some inaccurate and distorted reporting concerning the Hispanic problem during recent weeks. In spite of the press limitations, I can tell you that I have not and am not accusing you of breaking agreements. Thus far I have consistently credited you with good intentions, even when discomforted by some of your actions. I have not attempted to interfere in your area of responsibility.

In concluding let me repeat that I regret that you have been distressed. The report in question was less than accurate. You have not been accused by me of breaking agreements. I believe you do keep your promises. With kindest regards to both you and Brenda. . . .

The harm was done, however. Another brickbat had been handed over to my critics. First, I had broken my word to my fellow bishops. Second, I had jumped the gun on the next convention, where the issue of homosexuality would have been decided as had the ordination of women. The answers, of course, were complicated. First of all, there was no canonical barrier to a priest's sexual preference as there had been to gender. And who is to say who is a homosexual, since sexual preference is on a spectrum from total heterosexuality to total homosexuality. Where do you draw the line— one experience as a teenager, recent practice, promises to get professional help, promises never to be a bad boy again? How do you act on things heard in confidence, rumors, photographs, confessions with or without a lawyer present? How do you find any workable definition on the basis of human behavior and justice? Furthermore, ordination of someone known by a bishop to have homosexual tendencies had occurred many times, but the knowledge had been kept confidential. What I could be sure of, however, was that my rather tenuous relationship with Jack Allin had become even more frayed after the ordination of Ellen Barrett.

Bishop Allin's press conference was not the only thing to muddy the already polluted water. *Time* magazine printed an article with a photograph of Ellen, titled "The Lesbian Priest." It was a rather nice photograph of a smiling Ellen in her vestments. I received one copy with "tarnished" across the photo, another with "SICK, SICK, SICK, SICK," scrawled across it in red ink. The story ran as follows:

The Episcopal Church, which has just begun ordaining women as priests, added a new twist to that innovation last week. New York City's liberal Bishop Paul Moore ordained the Rev. Ellen Barrett, 30, the denomination's first openly committed homosexual priest of either sex. In an unusual last-minute plea to prevent the action, Colorado's Bishop William Frey had wired Colleague Moore: "Ordination of practicing homosexuals does not represent the mind of the church and is plainly contrary to the teachings of Scripture which we have all sworn to uphold."

During Barrett's ordination service, another priest, James Watt-ley, spoke out against it as a "travesty and a scandal." Moore answered that "many persons with homosexual tendencies are presently in the ordained ministry," and that Barrett was "highly qualified intellectually, morally and spiritually to be a priest."

Barrett, who has been studying for a doctorate in social ethics at the Graduate Theological Union in Berkeley, goes somewhat beyond "homosexual tendencies." She has said candidly that her relationship with her lesbian lover "is what feeds the strength and compassion I bring to the ministry." She also believes that "homosexuality is an alternative life-style that can be a good and creative thing."

The last paragraph became an issue in itself, and one of the hardest to deal with. First of all, Ellen denied having made the quote about her "lover." *Time* insists she did, that they have the transcript of the interview. In any case, the Standing Committee of my diocese and I were not aware of any interview at the time Ellen was approved for ordination. She was approved by me and the Standing Committee on the basis only of her admitted orientation, not her so-called "practice." Indeed, her personal character and behavior were never criticized nor brought to our attention by anyone as warranting criticism.

After the article came out, I was bombarded with the questions: "Is she or isn't she a practicing homosexual? Why don't you ask her? Why don't you find out?" At this point I become incensed. I have always refused to discuss with anyone the personal life of any of my clergy. I just don't do that. Our conversations are on the highest level of confidentiality. If this were not so, then I would resign as bishop tomorrow. But it is terribly difficult to uphold the right to privacy and confidentiality without sounding as though one were covering something up.

Another question was, Why didn't Ellen ask *Time* to retract the quote? Why didn't she sue? First of all, that would have been an impossible legal tangle, and, secondly, I believe she felt it was better to let it be. She also may not have felt it appropriate to thereby imply a criticism of "practicing" homosexual persons. In any case, my reply to such questions was always, "Ask her."

Nevertheless, it was widely assumed that we had ordained someone who had declared publicly that she was a practicing homosexual. The reality was that this had never been at issue when the committee and I made our decision to ordain. Muddy waters!

Letters from clergy and lay persons around the country were fascinating. Almost without exception they were written from emotion, not reason. They wrote as parents, churchmen, friends, colleagues, and simply feeling human beings. Their viewpoints were backed by Scripture, theology, politics, psychology, ecumenical or ecclesiastical concerns. But always their arguments were used as instruments, sometimes weapons, to express the emotion which motivated them, although each was convinced, I am sure, that he or she was expressing objective reasoning from which the position was taken. Religion and sexuality arise from the deepest level of our beings, the unconscious, the subrational, the suprarational. At best the statements were intuitive, a mixture of reason and sensitivity, at worst, raw emotion, even passion.

I have selected parts of letters that came in from people other than bishops, and mostly from outside the Diocese of New York. About half are supportive, half critical. As far as the breakdown between supportive, and critical among all the letters and wires I received, I would say that about three times as many were critical as supportive. The first rush was almost entirely "con," and then, after a few weeks, it evened out pretty well. The following excerpts are selected because of their special interest, substance, or humor—"black humor" in some cases. Some moved me to tears with their tenderness, others embarrassed me with their praise, others

were extremely upsetting. Much of the criticism spoke of
our action in driving people away from the Church. Others
said it drew them to the Church:

The problem is not that they [homosexual persons] necessarily
deny God, just the church. In fact, some of the strongest Christians
I know won't go to church because they feel that they are hated,
feared, and despised by their fellow "Christians." And to a great
extent, this is true. I do some counselling to the local gay popula-
tion. Word is getting around that there is a church in town that
cares enough to look past the neon label to the person behind
it. And they want to hear about Christ. They want to go to church
and be in a Christian atmosphere. This is a tearing need for them,
a very painful void in their lives. Given the chance to be welcome,
many of our churches would blossom into vibrant, growing bodies
with the help of these talented, caring people.

What you and Rev. Barrett had the courage to do is part of
the answer for these people, these children of God. They needed
more than words, they needed actions. Now I can point and say,
"Look, it's true." You have made my work and Christ's work more
evident. For this I thank you.

When I heard of the ordination of Ellen Barrett to the priesthood
it was as if at last there is someone willing to give another person
a fair shake regardless of sexuality.

. . . Speaking as a gay individual, the ordination has given me
a better feeling about the gay situation as whole, and more impor-
tantly an inner feeling that truly I am a child of God, regardless
of my sexual orientation.

I received an anonymous letter which I am going to quote
in its entirety because of the depth of feeling expressed. I
wish I knew who wrote it. I would like to meet him (her?)
and say, "God really does love you and so do I. Don't, please
don't hate yourself."

I telephoned NBC after watching you on the *Today* show to in-
quire about your address. They didn't have it, so I telephoned
your Diocese and took the liberty of requesting it. I do hope you
do not mind.

I seldom have the opportunity of watching *Today* for I leave
my home every morning at 6:45 to travel to work. I usually listen
to the radio for news, weather reports, etc.

However, this A.M. some force (I guess) pushed me near my TV set in the bedroom and I turned it on. I was met by Tom Brokaw who was just beginning to talk about you and the position of your church and homosexuals.

Curiosity aroused me and I listened and waited for you to appear. Normally, or usually I should say, I would not have listened for I have been rather tired of all the discussion shows in Miami relating to homosexuals. But I did listen.

You did something for me and it's very difficult for me to explain, but I will try. I am a homosexual and have been for most of the years of my young life. I don't know why I am, I only know I am. I'm rather ashamed of it, do not flaunt it and for that matter, hardly anyone knows of it. But the point is I am.

My only great hope and inspiration has been the Lord, but I have left him and the Church over a year ago. I am not a better person as I once was and there is a reason for it.

I heard Anita Bryant lecture one day about a year ago or so, and after her talk I realized that God disliked me. I felt horrible and so ashamed but there was nothing I could do. I was, I thought, a good Christian. I never bothered anyone, harmed or hurt anyone. I felt God was my partner for life, but after so many people have openly expressed their hatred for us poor wretched souls, I felt I was no longer clean.

But today I saw a tiny light at the other end of a very long tunnel and I heard your voice. You were kind about us, you didn't condemn us as so many people do. You didn't cry how sinful we were. You were honest and so sincere about the position of your church and the homosexuals and above all, you were so *right.*

The church should be able to make their own decision on whom should be ordained—whether they are homosexuals or not. And I whole-heartedly agree with your thoughts that an open, *practicing* homosexual should not be elevated to a position of a clergyman.

Nevertheless, it was the way you said all that. You didn't show hate for us. Listening to you made me feel good. It almost makes me feel that I should stop on the way home from work and visit with the Lord again. I do miss him.

I don't know what else to say, but with all my heart I am so grateful that "something" pressed me into turning the TV set on this morning and hopefully renewed my life again. Thanks, Rev. Moore—I only wish I were closer to touch your hand.

A gay activist, inured to the difficulty of his role, wrote me this touching letter about the interview on the *Today* show:

My Baptist mother called me on Monday in tears to state how much your appearance on *Today* had meant to her. She was raised to feel very guilty about her offspring, and her fundamentalism continues to keep her very troubled. Only by exposure on such a secular forum could you have ever reached her, as her church would never allow your position any exposure.

Let me stress my strong personal thanks for your courageous witness. I love my parents very dearly and they also love me very much. That you have made it easier for them to enjoy that love is a gift richer than all the money the Church could ever hope to lose by standing fast to the original such gift two thousand years ago. Thank you, my brother, for being a bishop like unto our heavenly bishop. May God give you full joy in your witness.

Several letters like the following arrived, which spoke of people being turned away from the priesthood because of homosexuality.

Stick to your guns—you have taken a brave stand for the rights of women and gays. We love you and miss you here in D.C.

I left the Church and my postulancy years ago over the homosexual issue. I didn't realize then that there were men like you in the Church.

Fight on with love and peace!

The variety of the response was heartening. The writer of this letter sees the issue straight, and from the perspective of a minority person who sees through pretense and knows the moral priorities in her life:

I read the *Daily News* on Tuesday, January 11, 1977 regarding Rev. Ellen Marie Barrett's ordination to Episcopal priesthood. I was very happy about it for many reasons. One of them being that she is a woman and I thought she wouldn't make it because of that, and two, because she is gay. I admire her courage and many courageous persons who have brought homosexuality out of the closet and into the open. I used to fight very hard myself, and am gay. I have found through experience that black people are not as courageous as whites. They want certain things and are miserable when they can't get them, but are too afraid to make the necessary sacrifices even if those sacrifices require going to jail or whatever. I tell them time and time again that Dr. King was thrown in jail and bitten by many a dog in order for us as blacks to get the few freedoms we have today, but still they are scared and always say that someone else will do it. And

it's about time they stopped leaving it to others and did it themselves.

On the other end of the spectrum were the inevitable letters
filled with anger and obscenity. Some described every part
of the anatomy of either sex in the most colloquial of terms
and identified me with them all in one way or another. Here
are a few bordering on the obscene, the insulting, the hilari-
ous, and the sick.

You are a stupid ass—and your stupidity is only exceeded by
the way you vilified our beautiful church.

I have been an Episcopalian for seventy years and have five generations of priests in my family, but it will be a long time before I
will be able to take the cup without feeling that you have desecrated
it.

What you did last week has made the devil one happy man.

A Chinese journalist said to one of your journalists when former
President Nixon was first in China, "You are very sexually oriented
in the United States. China was sexually oriented during the Ming
dynasty and the Ming dynasty fell."

This individual action on the part of Bishop Moore is understandable since it boldly exemplifies the presence of still another eastern
establishment prelate within the Anglican Communion bereft of
both discipline and cerebral portfolio.

I do pray that this is one of those kind of weird happenings
that can only happen in America. [This from a New Zealand
correspondent.]

I trust that we both believe that good Christian men should
accept the full responsibility of and for their actions done in good
conscience and not leave the burden to others. In light of your
ordination of a certain young lady to the priesthood, St. Stephen's
has had close to four hundred dollars in pledges withdrawn to
date. I trust that you are willing to make up this loss for a struggling
parish.

I do admire your courage in taking the step that you did and
appreciate your accepting the financial responsibility of your
actions.

[My reply to the above letter:

I feel a parish under the wise, Christian leadership of someone like yourself would certainly want to donate four hundred dollars to the mission of the Church in the inner-city of New York. If you should feel so moved then I would be delighted to take full financial responsibility for the effect of my action upon your parish.]

"And they cried with a loud voice saying, How long, O Lord, holy and true, doest Thou not judge and avenge our blood on them that dwell on the earth?" (The Saints in Heaven speaking to Christ, Revelation 6:10)

Once again the Bishop of New York has escaped the men in white jackets with butterfly nets. This time we were treated to the spectacle of a Bishop of the church "ordaining" a lesbian to the Holy Priesthood. As if this were not bad enough, she (?) went on national television and flaunted it before the world.

We are thereby left with several valid conclusions.

A. The Bishop of New York is a degenerate.
B. The Bishop of New York is insane.
C. The Bishop of New York doesn't care.
D. The Bishop of New York is a radical revolutionary.

Pick one or all of the above.

Question: Is this what the glorious saints of the Church died for? Did they die in order for us to run amuk?

Obviously, if this sort of thing continues, Sodom and Gomorrah can not be very far behind. We will have no one to blame but ourselves.

How long, O lord, how long?

From out here in the boondocks we peasants are getting a somewhat alarming view of Morningside Heights, where, in an unfinished Gothic cathedral in a doomed and lawless city, homosexual priestesses say the Mass in a language understanded of the people, while a bishop, ever attentive to the *Village Voice*, decrees that the only sin remaining to twentieth-century persons is to be a business leaving New York. We look forward to sermons dealing with Divine Grace inherent in sodomy and day care centers staffed by male homosexuals dressed as nuns (medieval drag, as it were).

Several organizations, not only churches, wrote to me or passed resolutions. I was especially pleased to hear from the Alliance to End Repression in Chicago, signed by the executive coordinator, Sister Gabriel Herbers, from a Midwest group of women lawyers, and of course from many gay rights groups. These people clearly saw that the ordination of a homosexually oriented person who was qualified constituted a statement for civil rights.

Some churchmen, even from conservative dioceses, were so upset with their local authorities who were critical of me that they issued circular letters supporting the action.

Episcopal clergy by and large are a rather decent group of people. They work for almost nothing, no longer have security, and spend their lives trying to help people and endeavoring to build their churches, usually against great odds. However, some of them wrote angry letters letting me know in no uncertain terms that I should be deposed:

Your ordination of an avowed lesbian as a priest in the Episcopal Church is the most outrageous and destructive action that any bishop could take at this troublesome time; it is doing irreparable damage to what was, to millions of us, the finest church in the world. . . .
I suggest that you resign as Bishop of New York and as a priest, and accept a position as a social worker (if you can get one); that is apparently the type of thing you would enjoy and Episcopalians throughout the United States would no longer have to apologize for your holding what was a respected post in God's Church.

. . . The Bible teachings shall stand. You, as a bishop of the Church, vowed to uphold its teaching. You have read but refuse to accept the plain truth that homosexuality is an abomination. Therefore you have been derelict in your duy to God. Because you have willfully, and with full knowledge, pursued your own way against His Word I feel you should be unfrocked and prevented from representing yourself as one of His apostles.

Naturally many clergy were sympathetic. One letter came from an older woman recently ordained and trained as a lawyer. She had known Ellen at seminary:

For some time I have intended to write you and express support and sympathy for your courageous stand in ordaining Ellen Barrett and admiration for her courage in wanting to be ordained before God as *herself*, thus openly declaring her sex preference before being ordained to the Diaconate. I know that you are getting the expected reaction of the purists and Pharisees, those pompous and self-righteous who are so uncertain of their own identities they must repeat the history of the 17th century witch-hunts and inquisitions. They have a peculiar interpretation of Jesus Christ, I must say.

Dear Ellen—I observed her for two years as a fellow student, and she was so determined not to "compromise" her sisters at Seminary, she suffered her difficulties *alone,* without letting the rest of us minister to her or share some of her burden. One could see the raw agony in her face—and I am so grateful you rescued her ministry from heartbreak. I think you gained the strength from your earlier agony with the first wave of women irregularly ordained priests. . . .

Some of the critical letters could not be brushed aside as hysterical or prejudiced, because they were serious and substantive. Reading one of these, particularly if it was from someone whom I respected and admired, gave me pause.

Unless I am mistaken, our Church still holds generally that the intention to practice fornication and adultery would render a man morally unfit for Holy Orders. It certainly has been the practice, at least until recently, to deny ordination to men who have been involved in a homosexual lifestyle, and I mean by this someone who is engaged in such acts and not simply someone who has temptations in this direction. Should not more discretion be used with regard to the decision to ordain someone, man or woman, who has made a public profession of homosexuality? Perhaps Miss Barrett is leading a chaste life. If so, then it seems to me that as her Bishop and for the sake of preventing public scandal, you might be wise to clarify this to the press so that the public will understand better than they do the whole issue.

I do not believe that the issue of public scandal is out-dated. Nor do I believe that people should be denied ordination solely on the grounds of their particular temptations. The Christian faithful, however, do have a right to expect their clergy to live in accordance with the Gospel when it comes to sexuality. We all have enough sinfulness and brokenness which cause offense to the faithful and the unbelieving public without intensifying the scandal by ordaining persons who the public could only too easily believe are guilty of moral turpitude.

I appreciate your concern for a Christian and humane treatment of all people who are tempted in the direction of homosexuality.

It is one thing to accept people in their brokenness; it is another thing to say that the brokenness is really wholeness. I do not believe that it was your intention to say this, but I am afraid that your comments about Miss Barrett have led vast numbers of people to think that this is what you believe. Surely it is incumbent upon all of us, living as we do in any age of immense sexual confusion, not to add to this confusion by public statements or actions which could too easily be misunderstood or misinterpreted by the public.

I sometimes wish that the Church could cure the confusion which seems to many to be the cause of divorce, of an increase in homosexuality, and of permissiveness toward pornography by stating, "Orgasm only within marriage," period. This may well be what the world *should* be like, but it simply is not a standard that many seem to be able to adopt for life. Few pastors I know would counsel a divorced man of thirty to remain celibate for the rest of his life. Until recently this was the implication of the Church's teaching. About five years ago the marriage canon was changed, so that people could remarry if it could be ascertained that they had tried seriously to keep their former marriage together and if they were firm in their purpose that the second marriage be life-long. This is an almost universally approved change of recent years and it was approved because it was informed by the forgiving and compassionate mind of Christ as well as by realism in regard to the world. Although I do not know the final answer to homosexuality, I do not see how a young man who, through no fault of his own, finds his sexual preference directed toward another man can be asked to be celibate all his life. It would seem to me more compassionate and realistic to have the Church help him work out a responsible relationship than to leave him in a perpetual state of guilt or to make him leave the Church. A rigid view in this matter, it seems to me, divorces the teaching and pastoral ministry of the Church from thousands who need and want it. And if a flexible approach like this makes moral sense for a lay person, should a priest be subject to a "higher" standard?

The following letter states the traditional position expressed above:

> You speak of "sexuality as a good and desirable way of expressing a loving relationship between persons." If by sexuality you mean sexual expression to orgasm, it is clear again from three thousand years of Jewish and Christian history and from the writings of all of the moral theologians up to the present that this is something which is to be practiced only between married persons. All other expressions of sexuality to orgasm are sinful. It seems incredible to me that I even have to argue this point for it has been accepted by all theologians within Judaism and Christianity until the second half of the twentieth century. I see no indication that the Holy Spirit is leading us to any other view.
>
> It is true that between married persons acts of sexual intercourse to orgasm need not and should not necessarily lead to procreation. Sexual expression *to* orgasm may be used as a human expression of love—but only within the married relationship.
>
> You, sir, have been grossly delinquent in your role as a defender of the Faith. Possibly an inhibition on your part of Ms. Barrett, a public statement of apology and confession of error, and/or your resignation will be enough to help to rectify your egregious fault. Failing these, I believe that you could successfully be prosecuted for conduct unbecoming a bishop. I would trust then that either clergy or laity in your own diocese or at least three bishops, according to the canonical rule, would cite you for your action and bring you to trial. You have caused a scandal in the Church and have caused many in my own parish to fall by the wayside. You have caused the little ones to stumble; you will recall that our Lord had something to say about those who did this.

Many Christians believe that homosexuality can be changed by prayer and spiritual healing. I accept the principles of spiritual healing and have seen several dramatic instances of the influence of prayer and the sacraments on mental or physical illness. I believe it is also possible that this healing process could lead to psychological change in the area of sexuality with some people. I think this would depend not only on their faith but also upon the dynamic whereby they came to be homosexual (and this is still a mysterious field) and *how* homosexual they were. Many persons are bisexual and can be pulled away from one course and set on another. Some adopt homosexuality, it is thought, because of a fear of women coming out of a conflict with their mother. If this fear can be resolved, the natural heterosexuality underneath can assert itself.

One letter I received gave a formula for spiritual healing:

We have seen several turn to Christ and by His power extricate themselves from their dilemma. It is never easy, but with God's help it is possible. The following formula has been used with several individuals:

1. Accept Christ as Lord and Savior of your life.
2. Face homosexuality or lesbianism as a sin (Rom. 1:26, 27, 32).
3. Confess it as sin (I John 1:19).
4. Ask God to break the habit pattern (I John 5:14, 15).
5. Walk in the Spirit through daily reading of the word of God, and submit to its teachings (Gal. 5:16–25; Eph. 5:17; Col. 3:15–17).
6. Avoid contact with all former homosexual friends.
7. Avoid places where such people gather.
8. Cultivate wholesome thought patterns; never permit your mind to visualize deviant or immoral behavior (Phil. 4:7).
9. Find a strong Christian friend who has never had this problem, one with whom you can turn for help when the temptation becomes strong.

The letter concludes:

I do not plan to support a denomination that condones the work of Satan.

On the other hand, I have known many conscientious homosexuals who have prayed, sought healing, made confessions, gone to psychiatrists, and still were left the same sexual emotions and feeling that it was their fault. A therapist wrote, "I have seen psycho-pathological denial and eventual disillusionment (and even suicide) on the part of those for whom it was claimed 'God had turned them into ex-gays'! "

Another kind of reason for homophobia is also difficult to deal with. This has to do with people who have had
unfortunate experiences like the one that is recounted in this
letter:

As far as the fact that she [Ellen] is a lesbian: As a mother whose
children are now taking an actual part in the Church, who are
encouraged by both parents in hopes of learning more truth, I
am sickened. I speak from first hand experience with lesbians. I
attended a woman's college on full scholarship. My roommate and
I were both class officers, freshman class. Midway through the year
we were threatened by upperclasswomen to "turn the freshman
class their way," telling us they were lesbians. Neither my roommate
nor I had any knowledge of what that meant! We turned them in
to the college president and received such brutal threats we had
to finish our exams under police protection. We were both able
to leave that school after exams. When we returned several months
later to retrieve belongings left behind in haste we noticed that
some of the girls who had lesbian roommates (as was disclosed
during the crisis) and who had not been able to convince their
parents to let them transfer to another college, had succumbed
to their peer pressure and had become lesbians themselves. As
fantastic as this may seem to you, it is the truth. I will never believe
that a deviant is only interested in its own kind. I believe that (as
evidenced by your new priest) they will attempt conversion at any
time and take pleasure in doing so.
   I see this ordination as mockery, a real danger and critical to
the survival of decency. There are, as I have discovered in my
quest for truth, some things that must not be tolerated, some actions that cannot be erased, some pain that never goes away and
some standards that must remain if we are to remain. I pray that
you will rethink your logic, that in your zest to prove your tolerance
you will consider the long range effects that are more important
than you or any mortal.

Such a person might find it hard to believe that such seduc-
tions and even child molesting occur with as much if not
more frequency among heterosexuals.

I would not want anyone to think that only those critical
of the ordination had a sense of humor. I quote from a supportive letter which is a little on the raunchy side, as they
say.

Your action in this case is especially ironic to me in that even though I have been told that I would be a qualified candidate for Holy Orders, I might just as well forget it. My bishop is not only anti-women's ordination but a homophobe who, when he has had too many, is wont to rail on about all the faggots in the church. This unfortunately one evening at a cocktail party prompted me to tell him precisely where he could stick his crozier.

Friendly letters came in from grandmothers, a black priest in California, Roman Catholics, psychologists, professors, a naval officer, and a rabbi:

I am very much interested in the organization "Integrity" and would appreciate knowing how to get in touch with the Rev. Ellen Barrett, who was recently ordained by you in New York City, with a view to learning more about the position of the Episcopal Church with respect to these people who have different feelings from what has been generally acceptable and accepted.

I can assure you that it is only in an effort to get my own seventy-year-old viewpoint open to understanding and acceptance of my own problem.

This is a thank you letter from a stranger. It would be perhaps proper and officious to say I'm a Roman Catholic associate pastor, or one of several Dignity chaplains here in Chicago, or the founding Moderator of the Gay and Lesbian Coalition of Metropolitan Chicago, or a member of our priests' Senate, or just a gay activist; but none of those are the real reasons I'm writing you. The reason is because you are one more in a lengthening line of Episcopal clergy persons who have the courage to make Christian values a reality within my life. I am alive, happy, and ministering as a priest today because you and others before you have given me real witness to Jesus. Thank you. Thank you for ordaining Ellen Barrett as my sister priest.

I suppose that I could be considered very "straight." I am a Lieutenant in the U.S. Navy; married to a devoted wife; am twenty-seven years old; a Conservative in basic theology, but very evangelical in putting it into action in the liturgy. Furthermore, I am a qualified Master of Ceremonies in all of our "High Church" rituals. . . .

I don't even know you, but I love you and I admire you for the actions that you have taken. I only wish that we could work together to Christianize our Episcopal Church, and make it reflect the *real catholic* intentions of Christ. . . .

From a rabbi:

I just wanted to tell you that I am in complete support of your ordination of Ellen Barrett. I feel that in 1977 sexism in all its forms should really be a thing of the past.

And a friend with crusty humor wished me well and recalled Bishop Pike:

I read Stringfellow's life of Jim Pike recently—comforting to see how you were lined up with the Good Guys in the House of Bishops—and found it very moving. Now you are a lot saner than old Jim—I don't want to push this analogy too far—but I think you are another pioneer catching the flak for the same reason; not because the trail you are pointing out is the wrong one, but just because it hasn't been traveled. Jim looked beautiful in that book, and you will too. Got to be.

Now maybe you don't need any support, in which case I hope no harm is done. By God, though, someone had to do these things, and you did them. A lot of people are more proud of you than ever.

This reminds me of a joke that Harry Golden tells about Irving Adler, the great matinee idol of the Yiddish Theater in New York. Apparently he was hell with the women. One night a good-looking girl with a good-looking baby boy turned up in his dressing room.

"Uh, Adler, don't you remember me? You took me to dinner when you were home a year ago. This is your son."

Adler congratulated her on the fine-looking baby and gave her two tickets to the performance. This obviously didn't satisfy her.

"Mr. Adler, your family needs bread," she said.

"You need bread, screw a baker," Adler said. "From me you get tickets."

I was hoping to use this at a diocesan convention—you know, what the hell did you expect from Moore—but, what the hell, I probably won't get the chance.

Keep the Faith.

And from a childhood friend:

This is not a followup to my last letter but quite simply a brief "fan" letter. Perhaps long overdue. You see, right after you made Church history by ordaining that lady (the "first lesbian," etc.) I happened to meet and have dinner with a young man who teaches English—and writes—and is in AA—and who attended the recent service and meeting of Integrity at which you presided. He said to me that you were quite simply magnificent and that everyone there felt you had "made Church history"—again?

Somehow both these moments in your life (coming so close together) have made me think back to the earliest days of our friendship and of how utterly impossible it would have been to predict—sitting at Granny Moore's mahjong table—some of the momentous and fascinating bypaths in which your life has travelled. And how proud your beloved Granny—not to mention your Uncle Len—would have continued to be of you.

So—I just had to tell you today how profoundly I admire you (as if you didn't know).

My feelings in reading all these letters are summed up in a note on the back of a greeting card: "Yes, the Episcopal Church is having a difficult time, but what better way than to be concerned about people! I am proud to be an Episcopalian."

11

The Diocese of
New York Speaks

Letters from bishops, resolutions from faraway dioceses, and letters from around the world were interesting and sometimes disturbing, but the negative reaction in my own beloved diocese was deeply worrying and extremely painful. One of the questions asked of a bishop at the time of his consecration is: "Will you maintain and set forward, as much as shall lie in you, quietness, love, and peace among all men?" The answer: "I will so do, by the help of God." Certainly Ellen Barrett's ordination had not set forth peace and quietness in the Diocese of New York. I was accused of sacrificing the unity and strength of the vast majority for the sake of a small minority. True, very true. And yet there was the parable of the lost sheep, not strictly applicable, but fairly close in spirit to what I had done.

I had always had this trouble in my ministry except in Jersey City, where the more radical I was, the better the people liked it. Since then I have been in conflict between doing what I thought was right and not rocking the boat. How do you balance speaking out on civil rights and alienating conservatives who, if cultivated, would give money to help minority social service organizations? Did I have a right to jeopardize the mission of our church in poverty areas by taking a stand on the homosexual issue? In a diocese as varied as ours one could hardly do anything without displeasing some. Inaction, I knew, would displease everyone.

It is like watching, feeling, a storm coming up on a summer afternoon. A drop or two of rain, distant thunder, skies darkening. You feel it in your insides if it is going to be a big one. The Barrett ordination had all the signs of a storm. Before the event, the mounting media excitement; after the event, the phone ringing, ringing, ringing. My assistant, Mrs. Lucila Woodard, looking worried but trying to be cheerful. Archdeacon Bob Willing from the northern part of the diocese calling in, saying, "Boss, I hate to bother you, but things are beginning to look a bit sticky up this way. I had lunch with a group of the clergy today and they say they are getting it from their people." Bishop Wetmore and Bishop Wright, my suffragans, looking concerned. "Maybe it will blow over," I say hopefully. Usually the response is, "Yeah, it probably will." But this time it was, "Not this one, I'm afraid."

I have been through enough to be able to handle my emotions fairly well. This time it was different. I found myself waking up at five A.M. and worrying, having Walter Mitty fantasies of going on national television to explain, or having a sound truck travel around the diocese, or saying to hell with you and resigning. I wrote a hundred statements in my head in those sleepless hours and said a hundred prayers. I called Ellen to commiserate over the flak she was receiving. I called Bishop Kim Myers of California, where Ellen lived, to see how things were going with him. I found no way out of my dilemma except to ride it through, heading straight into the waves.

Rumors as well as letters came to me. Parishes were withholding their assessments, some were thinking of leaving the Episcopal Church. One priest had called me a heretic from his pulpit. I began to see some of the statements made by my clergy. Some felt they had to tell their people they differed with me. Others defended me. One long, reasoned letter concluded:

Having spoken my piece, I must also add that as strongly as I feel on this matter, I feel more strongly still that this is my Church, this is my Diocese, and you are my Bishop. Though I disagree with your ordination of Ellen Barrett, and though I am hurt by it and even disappointed in your leadership, I value too strongly my right to say this ever to leave the Church or withdraw my support.

This from a bright, earnest, dedicated priest whose integrity and loyalty were unquestionable.

The rector of one of our large Manhattan parishes, Alan Houghton, published a commonsensical statement, which, while not in total agreement, was supportive:

Paul Moore may be guilty of questionable judgment but certainly is not lacking in compassion or courage. Frankly I do not know what I would have done under the circumstances nor am I bold enough to second-guess the decision of the person who had to make it. He was faced with a problem, a person and the mandate he carries to be fair and do what is right. He made a decision and by doing that forced us to face a reality which probably makes many of us uneasy and uncomfortable. . . .

Priests, doctors, lawyers, teachers, in fact all who are in the public view are expected to keep their private idiosyncrasies to themselves. Some drink too much or are unfaithful. Some use other people for their own designs or treat their families shabbily. Some teach things which aren't true or cheat people out of their dignity and rights or, even worse, some mouth things they don't believe themselves. That is all private and "what the public doesn't know won't hurt them." That is also rank hypocrisy.

I don't pretend to understand lesbianism—but I would rather have an avowed lesbian as my priest than one whose public image didn't match her private one and whose prejudices and piety were too overbearing to meet me where I was and to understand what I might be struggling with deep within myself.

As the weeks went on, at least thirty parish vestries made resolutions. The first few were statements either for or against the ordination. About the third week after the event, I received the first resolution withholding assessment. This was a body blow, not just because of the money involved, which we needed desperately for our mission work, but because of principle. The assessment is a kind of tax which is levied on each parish according to its ability to pay. This allows a parish to stay in good standing in the diocese and to vote in the diocesan convention. To withhold it is a major act of rebellion. This was my first encounter with open rebellion. The first parish to withhold was The Church of the Holy Communion in Mahopac, Putnam County. About five years ago, they brought in a new rector, who was in the charismatic movement. The parish had begun to grow, but its theology had become strongly evangelical to the point of what seemed to me a biblical fundamentalism and preached a rigid moralism unusual in the Episcopal Church.

By the authority vested in us by the Episcopal Church of the Holy Communion of Mahopac, New York, and by our commitment as Christians, we write to express our strong opposition to the ordination of Ellen Barrett. On January 11, 1977 at the Annual Meeting of the Church of the Holy Communion, the congregation requested that the vestry take appropriate and immediate action to express opposition. At its meeting of January 18th, the vestry was in unanimous and prayerful agreement on the following [a long statement based on biblical test against homosexuality]. . . .
As Christians, we pray that Ellen Barrett will go through "the purifying waters" and come into the full grace of God's love.

A total of six parishes withheld their assessment; one in Dutchess County, two in Westchester County, one in Putnam County, one in Staten Island, and one in Manhattan. The Manhattan parish hit me hard because it was the parish from which I applied for postulancy in 1945, where I was married in 1944, and where my first child was baptized. The rector was a classmate and old friend.

I decided I had to take some action. I wrote a letter to

the senior vestrymen of every parish. (My earlier statement had gone to the clergy only.)

Dear Friends:

By now you've been battered by many communications on the ordination of Miss Ellen Barrett. I really want to write to you personally at this point to communicate as directly as possible my own feelings about it.

First of all, the tremendous publicity in reaction to this ordination was a total surprise. We had chosen and ordained Ellen to the diaconate about a year ago. There was some small amount of publicity but no great reaction. I thought her ordination to the priesthood would have even less reaction since she was already ordained a deacon. But for whatever reason, the papers and media took off on this event and the result is that we have a very difficult situation on our hands. Frankly, had I known that there would be such a reaction to it I certainly would have waited a while before ordaining her since I think we are catching a lot of the emotion generated by the ordination of women and even the new Prayer Book. But what is done is done and we need to live with it and deal with it.

As I said in my statement to the clergy, the Standing Committee and I decided to ordain Ellen after a long time of thinking and discussing the matter. It first came up as an issue for us at least five years ago and succeeding committees have discussed the matter of homosexuality and the priesthood over the years. What we decided to do was to take individuals as they came before us: we did not believe and do not believe that a person being candid about his/her homosexual orientation should be a bar *per se* to the priesthood. In other words, we chose Ellen Barrett as a person whom we thought worthy of ordination.

Another complicating problem is that her personal life did not come before us as an issue since it had never caused scandal. Since then she has been quoted by *Time* magazine and other sources as having discussed her personal life; she assures me she never has and that these quotations are false. However, once something hits the paper it is believed by many, no matter how many denials one makes of it.

In any case, I am terribly upset by the conflict that has ensued. I understand that a few of our parishes are even speaking of withholding the assessment because of this and other things they disagree with. This is really very wrong, I feel, because the assessment is the means by which the people in the parishes support the general mission of the Church. I don't really think a vestry has the right to make that offering impossible. Also I always think of our Church as a family, very dependent one upon another—and even if the family has a terrible fight the members still have to contribute toward its common support; otherwise the whole family is destroyed. Also the action, whether you agree with it or not, was taken canonically by the Bishop, having the Standing Committee and the Ministries Commission participating in the decision to ordain. The Standing Committee and the Bishop are your elected officers, given authority to do this. We may have made an error but we stayed within our authority. Withholding funds, however, is an uncanonical action (Diocesan Canon Seventeen).

But perhaps most important—withholding funds will hurt the ministry of our Church to the poor, the old, the sick, the young, and those who desperately need our help during these difficult times. No matter what you may think of me, I pray that you do not hurt such innocent persons because of a disagreement with me or any other bishop.

If any vestry wishes to discuss this matter further, please get in touch with me.

Let me conclude by saying how much I admire and respect the leadership which the vestries give to their parishes in this diocese, for the hundreds of hours you put in without recompense and the responsibility you hold. I hope you read this letter in the friendly tone in which it is written and take to heart some of the thoughts I have shared with you.

This brings my best wishes and blessings to you and your parish. Please remember me and the diocese in your prayers during these difficult times.

Through this period I received some letters from clergy who loved me but who were torn apart by all the conflict. Here is one from one of our very finest and most loving priests. Reading it made me wince with pain.

You were so kind to stay the night with us the other Tuesday and to share with us your thoughts, as we did ours. We enjoyed your visit very much and this concern has prompted me to share with you the feelings of our vestry meeting, held this past Tuesday. As Shakespeare would write, "I do love thee and it is my love that speaks."

As I told you, we are a very conservative parish. As I think was reported in the "Living Church," we are among the six percent of all churches that prefer the Book of Common Prayer and only have Holy Communion at eleven o'clock the first Sunday of the month, with Morning Prayers our biggest service. We have Holy

Communion every Sunday at eight A.M., but when this is celebrated at the later time, we have some fifty less attending, as we would at Morning Prayers. So in your midst you have a very conservative body of Christians and the majority of the vestry—not all—are worried "what you will be up to next."

We have about two members who would vote for you in relationship to your ordaining a lesbian. On the other extreme we have at least two, perhaps more, who would be glad if we stopped our funding. One man, and I must say a really devout man, is fighting within himself whether to leave the Church.

Although you say—and I am sure you meant it sincerely—Miss Barrett was treated by you as a person and not as a method of opening the door for all alternative style Christians to ordination. But of course, that is what it is. I must say, I join the majority of the vestry in deeply believing that homosexuals should not be ordained. My dear Bishop, recall the days when you were a Parish priest. My goodness what temptations there were to take advantage of some attractive girl, who in the toils of sorrow or despair opened her heart to the Parish priest? A person with severe personality disorders, as I view homosexuals, should not be put into this position of intimacy of trust and the lack of trust and fear of a homosexual priest is engendered into the Parish. This was so, here, with a previous rector.

I pray, so hard, that I will not lose any of my people —it breaks my heart to see them leave the Church, as so often, they go nowhere else. It would also grieve me terribly to have our vestry stop our funding. As you left in your Rover (one door would not open— as Dr. Tyler would say, "There is a sermon in that, boy") you said that you would try and be a good boy.

You know what some of our vestry see now? They see you as Isaiah in the Temple—St. John the Divine—marrying men to men, women to women, as they have so declared—homosexuals dancing around the throne crying "Holy, Holy, Holy" and our Bishop saying "Send me."

Dear Bishop, we are worried here and with breaths held awaiting the falling of the other shoe—please have mercy on us, for we are conservative sinners here.

We love you, very much as a person, but, for us, as a Shepherd you are so far off, please try and be gentle with us as we dearly want to follow you in our worship to God Almighty. God bless you and keep you.

P.S. I wrote this letter directly after our vestry meeting March 15th, but the Parish secretary has been so busy that she has only had time now to type it. Thank you so much for your letter of

March 15th. We love you dearly and our home is open to you and Brenda whenever you want a break from the cares of the Churches. And when you come we will not even mention the lady who has caused us all so much pain—whatever her name was!

Other clergy took the opportunity to preach on the subject or to draft formal statements pro and con. Of the comforting mail, I was especially touched by a poem, from a man I did not know:

FOR PAUL MOORE

Once it was simple:
Sacrifice to Caesar or
go feed the lions;
Like the Navy Cross—Mom's proud,
Bands play, you did the right thing.

Being a bishop isn't like that any more.
Martyrdom is hid
by that complex, crucified,
God, within the wrong issue.

The one that the Church
isn't quite ready for, now.
Salted with schism.
And you can't know if you're right.
A proper crucifixion.

Peter Steven Gannon

I was so pleased to receive the following from the little church where Ellen was ordained:

To the Rectors, Wardens and Vestries of the Diocese of New York:

In view of the controversy which has recently arisen concerning the ordination of The Rev. Ellen Marie Barrett by the Bishop of New York, The Right Reverend Paul Moore, Jr., we, the Vestry of the Church of the Holy Apostles, desire to make our position clear.

We continue to respect and admire Bishop Moore. While this ordination of Ellen Barrett to the priesthood has aroused profound controversy, we believe that this action was taken after prolonged consideration and deliberation, and in accordance with a deeply Christian conscience. We understand the Bishop acted after proper consultation with the governing bodies of the Diocese and in accordance with Canon Law.

We know the Bishop to be a good and faithful shepherd of his flock. He has been a strong supporter of our parish as he has of the other struggling inner city parishes in this Diocese. In conference with him we have always found him to be a good and wise counselor whose principal aim was the promotion of the mission of the Church.

Insofar as payment of the diocesan assessment and of the designated funding is concerned, we join the other parishes which have urged that these funds not be withheld. We have met and will continue to meet these obligations.

In conclusion, we reaffirm our loyalty to the Diocese and our support of Bishop Moore in the fulfillment of his Christian duties.

And my reply:

Dear Friends:

I can't tell you how supportive I found your resolution to be. If any Vestry in the Diocese should have been upset by the Barrett ordination it was you; instead, with your accustomed courage, tenacity, good sense and Christian charity you endured the slings and arrows of the press, the public and your fellow churchmen, as well as the invasion of the Bishop. It was a joyful and historic night, I still maintain, but sometimes amidst the flak it's hard to see the sun.

Keep up your courage. You are marvelous people! I believe sincerely that we did the right thing and that history will show that so to be. In the meantime let us continue to join hands to set forward the mission of the Church.

Blessings and much love.

The letter to the vestries and communications with the clergy did not quiet things down. Other measures needed to be taken. I decided to have two hearings, one in the Northern Region at Hyde Park, the other in Westchester County at White Plains. The clergy of the interparish councils in the city did not feel that a hearing was necessary in New York. City people, by and large, were not so upset as those in the suburbs. I suppose they are more used to hearing about, seeing, knowing homosexual persons. Or as in the case of the black and Hispanic churchmen, they have more important things to worry about, like unemployment, crime in their neighborhoods, the breakdown of the school system.

The format we decided upon for the hearings was a panel discussion and questions from the floor. The panel was made up of the president of the Standing Committee, a seminary professor, the psychiatrist used in examining postulants for holy orders, and myself.

We all drove up together to the first hearing through the cold night. I was nervous, afraid. Public meetings are a risk. Emotions can erupt. And yet I have always felt that if you do something you should be willing to defend it, whatever the price.

We approached the church where the meeting was to take place. Cars were parked for several blocks in each direction. My heart sank. People usually do not come out on a weekday winter night in any numbers. I saw some of the clergy whom I knew to be most upset. They avoided looking at me. I saw others who said hello and good luck. The parish hall was crowded, standing room only. People were even sitting on the stage opposite from the panel. There must have been three hundred people there.

At eight o'clock I arose. Silence came over the room. "The Lord be with you." Standing up, they responded, "And with Thy Spirit." I prayed for the presence of the Spirit. For forbearance, openness, calm, compassion. I prayed for the unity of the Church. I prayed that we be forgiven for what sins we might have committed.

The people sat down, and I began:

"We come together at a most difficult time, a time of change and conflict in the Church and in the world. All institutions are caught up in this change. The Church, if she is to be part of human life, should be caught up in the conflict and the change. Our Lord was. He was crucified by it. The church as the Body of Christ is scarred and torn as He was.

"Tonight we discuss a most emotional and personal issue, sexuality and religion. Because of the emotion involved I ask you to observe these general guidelines in debate. Stick to the subject. This is not a fight, but a discussion, an opportunity for us to learn from each other. Please do not indulge in personalities. I will refrain from that. In fact I will not discuss the personality or the private life of any of my clergy, including Ms. Barrett. The subject is: Should the bishop and Standing Committee have permitted the ordination of one who has admitted her homosexual orientation."

I reviewed the facts: Ellen's original application, turndown, reapplication, screening, and final ordination as a deacon and then as a priest. I mentioned the special meeting of the Standing Committee when we had been asked to refrain from ordination. I mentioned the clamor of the media. I reiterated that there had been no agreement to the contrary at the General Convention. I ended on a positive note, reemphasizing Ellen's qualities of dedication, honesty, and competence, and that we felt her candor about her sexuality was not a bar to ordination.

I then introduced the panel, each of whom spoke for a few minutes from his point of view.

Then came the questions. Many hands went up. On the right I recognized a group from one of the parishes that had withheld assessment. I called on a layman. He spoke with emotion and anger at the violence Ellen's ordination had done to the Church. A woman arose and spoke of her fear that a lesbian as a role model would be a bad influence on her child. Another woman went further and said she would not allow her child to go near such a person lest she be taken advantage of. Our psychiatrist quietly pointed out that homosexuals were no more likely to harm a child than other persons, and that a homosexual role model was not the cause of homosexual tendencies as far as could be determined.

A hand went up on the other side of the room. Someone there said he knew many fine persons, indeed fine priests, who were homosexual and that they had been effective pastors. Someone else said a person's private life was his or her own business. And so it went for about an hour. Finally, a priest sitting on the stage asked the question I had been anticipating with anxiety. It really was the ultimate question. When he stood up, the room fell silent, because they knew he was strongly on the critical side.

"Bishop Moore," he asked, "do you think homosexual activity is a sin?" Although I knew it would come, I had not really decided how I would answer. Although the Bible could be interpreted as being written in a different cultural and religious context, nonetheless both the Old and New Testaments explicitly state that homosexual practice is sinful. I could have avoided the question, since it was not an issue in Ellen's case at the time of ordination. I took a deep breath and said what I thought: "Sex can be sinful in both homosexual and heterosexual relationships. But it need not be so." The subject then changed to the Standing Committee's role in the process. It was getting late. I felt I should close the meeting. Then one of our clergy was recognized and turned to the audience and said, "I came into the Episcopal Church because I admired her liturgy and I felt the Episcopal Church was the true Catholic Church. I also came into our Church because it had bishops to act as pastors to their clergy. I regret to say that I can no longer accept Bishop Moore as my Father in God."

When I heard that, tears came to my eyes. I had a hard

time controlling myself. I was fond of this priest, and I felt
we were good friends. I admired him. I never had had anyone
say such a thing to me before. Above all else I wanted to
be a pastor, a friend, a father, if you will, to my clergy. I
don't remember much else of what happened after that. I
closed, a few minutes later, with a blessing. I really don't
recall how long it was before we were driving home. I was
still in a daze.

The next hearing, a few weeks later, was not quite as rough
as the first one. We added a woman to the panel, Sister
Andrea, the superior of one of our religious orders. She
has a fine sense of humor and in her remarks said that she
had not had many serious boy friends, but she finally found
the right one and that she was still with him. It took the
group a moment to get it. The laughter at Jesus being "the
right one" brought down the house. One addition to my
presentation that was helpful was telling the story of my
friend John, the priest who had introduced me to the Church
and who was later deposed.

After the hearings I received some friendly letters. Here
are two, one from a very active churchwoman, another from
a new member.

Thank you for last Tuesday night. It must have been deeply
painful for you. I wish some of us could have taken the suffering
for you. That meeting was certainly not an example of Christians
behaving in love, and I found it so ugly that I hurried out just to
keep from saying something hateful myself. But later at home I
found that what I had taken home with me was not that spirit of
petty anger, but the memory of your compassionate response to
everyone there—the feeling that you do belong to all your diocese
and cannot be kept from caring about them by anything they do
or say.

I came to the meeting because I have lingering doubts deep
down about a homosexual as a mentor or "hero" for my children.
Nothing factual that was said has changed those doubts. But they
are no longer important, because I suddenly *knew* that the only
way to handle the problem (if it *is* a problem) is by going into it,

knowing it, treating it with love and Christian caring, and trusting the Holy Spirit to work through it with us. Surely the Lord never taught us to *fear* another human being, as I saw fear on Tuesday night. At morning prayer today, the second lesson was Paul's letter to the Galatians, 5:16–26—it really says it all. I am very thankful for that Paul, and our Bishop Paul.

I have recently become a Christian (baptized last August by Father Blasingame at Grace Church). Being new to all this, I went to the meeting on Tuesday to see just why there is an issue—I was warned on my way in that I would be the only person in attendance with a liberal Jewish background. Well, it didn't take long for me to see what the issue is, and to see how dynamic an issue it is. When the meeting was over I was completely exhausted simply from listening (and caring). Someone asked me what I thought about it all, and all I could say was, "I didn't know it would be so hard to be a Christian." I am glad to be Christian—very glad to be part of a family which feels and thinks, and cares so much, so deeply.

We are a family. I understand a family to be a unit in which each member strives to support each other member. The joy of family is the strength which comes from knowing that the family will remain whole and united through hard times as well as good, through joy as well as pain, through agreements and disagreements. Now, I am an expert at family fights, an expert at stamping my feet. I have never stormed out. I have never threatened to leave the family in time of pain—that is when a family must, MUST stick together. How are we, as Christians, to be examples of God's love, if we cannot love each other? I am very pained, as I am sure you are, over some of the feelings which were shared on Tuesday.

Bishop Moore, I admire your wisdom in understanding the need for a meeting such as was held on Tuesday. I applaud your strength and courage to sustain that meeting in the calm and peaceful manner in which you did. And I am proud to be an Episcopalian in the diocese of New York, to have you, as a gift of God, as my spiritual leader and teacher. May God continue to grow within you and shine forth. God Bless.

P.S. I don't quite know what to make of this issue, but the way I see it, we are all trying our best to be the best Christians we can be, and Pop's not going to let us go too far wrong. It's a matter of Faith . . . and I have long since learned, if Pop really is against something, He's not going to let it happen, no matter what we think or do.

The months passed and things began to quiet down. I met with as many of the dissident vestries as I could. The discussions were along the same lines. One or two that were wavering decided to pay their assessments. Another that was withholding changed its mind under a new rector. I still hope that time will heal the wounds. Thank God, no congregation in my diocese decided to leave the Church as has happened in other dioceses.

The summer came. Vacation brought some perspective. The next event to prepare for would be the House of Bishops meeting in the fall of 1977.

12

What Is the Crime?

In the middle of the summer I had a call from the Presiding
Bishop. He said he would like to get together to discuss
the forthcoming meeting of the House of Bishops in Florida.
Jack Allin did not want a furor at the meeting any more
than I did.

Bishop Allin keeps a neat office. It is a corner room in
the headquarters building of the Episcopal Church on Second
Avenue and Forty-third Street. The room is bright, small,
unpretentious. In the distance is the United Nations; near
by, the Ford Foundation's extraordinary extravaganza of a
building. Somehow Jack Allin seemed out of place. A homier
study, somewhere in the South, would have been a more
congenial backdrop for his courteous Southern manner.

We sat down, passed the time of day. He said he wanted
to get to know me better, to understand me, before discussing
the particulars of the meeting. The conversation was friendly,
fairly candid, and rambling. What he could not understand
was why, from time to time, I did or said such controversial
things. I tried to explain. He said again, as he had said publicly
before, that I was an "idealist." This meant, I believe, that
I saw the world as better than it was, and the Church as
more sensitive than it was, and that these perceptions altered
my sense of reality. I felt this to be a rather charitable description from one for whom I had caused so much difficulty

over the years. In turn, I saw him as a person dedicated to reconciliation within the Church and bound and determined to move the Church forward. The Church's less than adequate response to questions of social justice did not seem to bother him as much as it did me. He trusted the Church to do the right thing. Our job as bishops, he indicated, was to unite and build the Church.

We met again a month or so later to talk specifics about the forthcoming meeting. The bishops' agenda committee had suggested that the meeting be opened by the two "controversial" bishops, Bishop Chambers, the schismatic bishop, and myself, each reading a statement. I did not like that a bit. "Jack," I said, "that would make it an *ad hominem* debate rather than one on the issues. Furthermore, I really resent being put in the same category as Al Chambers, who has endorsed a schismatic movement in the Church and goes around the country confirming in other people's dioceses without permission. We in New York have obeyed every letter of the canon law over the past several years, despite heavy pressure to do otherwise."

"Paul, I agree with you," he said. "What would you suggest?"

"Allow the Pastoral Committee to bring in its report. I have seen it. It's good. Then let all of us discuss the issues. At that point I will make a statement if it seems appropriate."

"That sounds good. I'll go with that. But, Paul, I really want to know how far you are willing to go toward compromise with the other side. If you could say you would not ordain any more homosexual persons until after the General Convention's report on sexuality in 1979, I think we could avoid a confrontation. These fellows have to have something to bring home to their dioceses. A lot of their people are pretty upset."

"I can't do that, Jack. I already intended to tell the 'brothers' how sorry I am that they have caught so much hell because of my action, and the tone will be conciliatory. I think I would be willing to say I would not ordain anyone who stated *publicly* that he or she was a *practicing* homosexual person. I cannot go further than that without going against my conscience and the stand of the Standing Committee of my diocese. It would also repudiate Ellen Barrett."

House of Bishops. September 1977. Brenda and I drove up to the Sandpiper Inn at Port St. Lucie, Florida, in the evening. It was, as they say, a garden spot. Palm trees over the lagoon, fountains splashing in fake Spanish courtyards, tennis courts, bars, swimming pools. Good taste, for that kind of place, but definitely luxurious.

I did not expect much action the night the convention opened. I was sitting at my desk, shuffling papers, in a large auditorium. The chairs were arranged on three sides of a rectangle, with the podium in the center. The gallery was just behind me. The Presiding Bishop was making his address. ". . . I cannot accept women in the priesthood. . . . They cannot be priests any more than fathers. If you are unwilling to have a Presiding Bishop with these views I would be willing to resign." I sat up with a start. I asked my neighbor, "Did he really say that!" My neighbor nodded.

It took us the whole week to deal with what seemed a very strange statement for the head of a church to make about his own ordained women clergy. The evening following the opening meeting was filled with conjecture, anger, bewilderment. Someone said to me, "At least that takes the pressure off you a little." "A hell of a way to have it happen," I replied. But of course he was right. The pressure was off to some extent.

The next day was full of reaction to the Presiding Bishop's address and other matters. On Saturday night Brenda and I, Kim Myers from California, and Otis and Elvira Charles from Utah went out to dinner. Kim, Otis, and Elvira are among my oldest and closest friends. We discussed the resolutions on homosexuality that had been submitted to the House. I was up for criticism, and Kim was the object of a resolution aimed at preventing him from licensing Ellen Barrett as a priest in his diocese. Kim had said that he was going to wait for the House of Bishops to meet before licensing her, in case they said anything to change his mind. The resolutions read:

Committee on Miscellaneous Resolutions (21)
Report No. 1
Subject: Resolution B-17

BE IT RESOLVED, that in view of the historic understanding of homosexuality by Christians and the Christian tradition, the House of Bishops states its strong disapproval of the unilateral action of the Bishop, the Standing Committee, and the Commission on Ministry of the Diocese of New York in conferring Holy Orders upon a person who is a professed homosexual and who advocates homosexuality as a legitimate life style.

Report No. 2
Subject: Resolution B-16

BE IT RESOLVED, that in view of the statement of the Bishop of California which seeks guidance from this House concerning the licensing in the Diocese of California of a professed homosexual person, it is the mind of the House that the same principles adopted by this House for such a person seeking ordination should be applied to any person seeking a license to officiate as an ordained minister of the Church.

We were weary. We griped and groused about the other bishops interfering with our business. Brenda had been silent. Now she broke in, "What's the matter with you tired old liberals, can't you find the energy for a fight anymore?"

We were galvanized. "What do you mean, 'tired old liberals'? We're still doing a lot."

"Are you going to let those conservatives run all over you?"

she said. "And how do you think Ellen will feel! It's too bad there aren't some women bishops in there. They wouldn't just sit on their benches."

"They sure wouldn't," says Elvira, joining the attack.

"Let's order dinner!" I reply. This is usually a safe retreat. It gets people thinking about what they want to eat, and by the time they decide, it's easy to change the subject.

There was no deterring Brenda. "Sure, why not? And what are you going to do about the resolutions?"

By the time the dinner was over, we had a strategy and had scheduled a meeting for the following night for bishops sympathetic to our side. We were off and running, just like the good old days.

The debate about Ellen's ordination began Monday morning. The resolution on the Diocese of New York was on the floor. One or two bishops spoke to it. Then I asked for the floor and read a prepared statement outlining the facts once again. We did not intend a test case, I said. We were not thereby commenting on the homosexual life style. The issue before us had been homosexual *orientation,* not practice. I was not going to discuss the personal life of Ellen Barrett, or of any of my other clergy for that matter.

We went into discussion groups for the rest of the afternoon. The reports from the groups the next day, by and large, disapproved homosexual marriage (a point raised by someone else). Ordination of homosexually oriented people was all right if they promised celibacy. I was called thoughtless in my timing, and it was stated that I had caused the Church enormous damage. Such an uproar, they said, had not occurred in recent memory. The Diocese of New York should be denounced. Heterosexual marriage was the norm for sexual activity of Christians.

After the reports, speakers arose, mostly to rehearse and embellish the points already made. One bishop said I had shown an "aristocratic disdain" for the rest of the Church in my action. Another said that what Al Chambers had done was nowhere near as upsetting to his people as my actions. Another said I had misled them by saying that Ellen was not a practicing homosexual, and then went on to quote the *Time* magazine article. The hair on the back of my neck began to prickle and finally I could stand it no longer. I got up again and read, with all the force I could muster, a paper that Brenda and I had prepared the night before:

I have been called to the mission of the Church in New York, that enormous, strange, desperate, vital city where the customs and the culture are so different from other parts of the country. It is not easy to relate to such a mission, to make any impression on such a city, to be heard in such a noisy place. However, from time to time, we have been heard there. From time to time, we have been able to lift up a sign of hope in that city.

One such sign of hope was the ordination of Ellen Barrett. It was not intended to be such, but because of the time at which it occurred and the media coverage it received, the city and the country came to know that we affirmed her candor, her courage, her honesty. When she was ordained, the gay community felt it to be a sign that the Church finally accepted them as human beings.

Do you realize that every gay person in America will be watching what happens here this week? Do you realize that if you officially condemn this ordination you will be casting a judgment upon the ministry of hundreds, perhaps thousands of bishops, priests, deacons, and lay persons of the Church who live with this problem? Do you realize that you will be removing a sign of hope they finally see in a church that has treated them so shabbily over the years?

We have shown great concern for the fifteen hundred church people at St. Louis. [This was a meeting of people who were considering leaving the Episcopal Church and setting up a schismatic church adhering to the old Book of Common Prayer and forbidding the ordination of women]. Have we no concern for this huge and most misunderstood of all minorities to which our brothers, our sisters, our children might belong? Gay people live in constant fear for their jobs, their homes, their very lives. You have no idea what this condition can mean in someone's life.

A priest who started me on my vocation lived a haunted, broken life because of the way the Church treated his homosexuality; and yet, were it not for him, I would not be here today.

No one of you dares deny the effective priesthood of homosexual clergy you have known. Are you about to say that the grace of priesthood cannot function in such persons when their effectiveness has been shown again and again?

If you censure or deplore the action of the Diocese of New York, you are deploring the priesthood of any homosexually oriented priest whatever his behavior; and you are insulting hundreds of the clergy of our Church.

Please carefully listen to the possible consequences of this proposed action. Aspirants for holy orders who sense a vocation within themselves will be encouraged to lie to their psychiatrist, Standing Committee, Ministries Commission, and bishop. Ordained clergy of the Church who have declared themselves to be gay will be left wondering when charges for deposition will be brought against them. The Episcopal Church may become the scene of a McCarthy-like purge, rife with gossip, charges, and counter-charges. Also the General Convention study process will be frustrated. It may result in many communicants leaving this Church.

Bishop Myers' and Bishop Corrigan's papers have set forth the deep reasons for not withholding orders from gay persons, reasons found in an understanding of the humanity of Jesus. I need not rehearse them here. But let me say that the sexuality of an ordinand is not what I am most concerned about. When I interview a person for the ministry, I try to see into his heart. I search for love, sensitivity, and courage in his dedication to our Lord Jesus. Of such qualities is priesthood made. The quality of courage has been sorely lacking in our Church of late. Perhaps courage is even more important than sexual orientation!

There has been much talk here about freedom of conscience. We have said in many comments that our own Presiding Bishop has a right to deny the action of the General Convention of the Church. Given this principle of freedom of conscience, do you then proceed to censure or deplore a Bishop and Standing Committee acting with full canonical scrupulosity in ordaining someone whom they believe qualified and whom most of you have never met? I think such an action is outrageous!

I have been a member of this House for almost fourteen years where, often with some difficulty of conscience, I have remained loyal to the doctrines, discipline and worship of the Episcopal Church, and to the so-called collegiality of this House. To be coupled for criticism or perhaps censure with a bishop who has flagrantly and often broken canon law, who is leading the Church into schism, makes me ashamed, humiliated, and brought to tears.

I have not broken any canon law. I have not been accused of

immorality. I have not been accused of making any heretical statement.

What is the crime? Am I being criticized for the remarks attributed to one of my clergy, after ordination, based on hearsay, and not made by me? I remind you that the ordination itself had nothing to do with sexual practice but only with admitted orientation. I also remind you that I was not called to task at the General Convention meeting of this House, by which time Ellen Barrett had been made deacon.

What is the crime? To attempt to bring the message and love of Christ to the great city of New York in a way that people outside the Church can understand?

In New York we are not ministering to the ideal American nuclear family. Instead our churches are full of divorcees, alcoholics, the aged, homosexuals, poor blacks, Puerto Ricans, Chinese, Haitians, immigrants—in a word the dispossessed. These are our people, God's children, the poor beloved of Jesus of Nazareth.

If this action [the ordination of Ellen Barrett] is formally disapproved, my brothers, I will feel that this House and I differ radically about what the meaning of our apostolic office is. Is it to manage, administer, and keep safe a steadily decreasing number of frightened and confused people; or is it to see the modern world as it is, and bring to that changing, suffering world the liberating, loving message of the Gospel of Christ.

That statement was well received. At last my main point that I had ordained an *admitted,* not *practicing,* homosexual seemed to have gotten through. Three notes came to my desk, the first two from fellow bishops:

Your statement was one of the most cogent and moving I have heard in the House. I am so grateful that the House simply put the motion out of consideration. I only wish the margin had been more overwhelming.

The only statement thus far in this meeting which touches on God's reality. Thanks.

The third was from Brenda, who had been sitting in the first row on the far left in a bright red dress:

Don't forget to ask Kim for drinks tonight. Here are your cigarettes. I'm very, very proud of you and, of course, love you madly.

An amendment to change the resolution from "states its strong disapproval" to "censures" followed. Censuring is the strongest statement against a bishop the House can make, and is seldom used. The amendment failed. Finally John Coburn, the new Bishop of Massachusetts, who had been in my diocese as a priest, went to the microphone.

"Gentlemen," he said, using a very low-key, shoulder-shrugging manner, "don't you think we are going a little far? I was on the Standing Committee of the Diocese of New York when Ellen Barrett was approved for ordination. The matter was just as the Bishop of New York has said. We went through the process of screening assiduously in complete accord with the canons. If the Bishop of New York stands to be censured, then as a member of that Standing Committee, so do I. But I simply do not see any reason on which such a motion can be based."

"Mr. Chairman, I move to table," someone said.

"Seconded." The motion to table is not debatable. It carried, sixty-six to forty-eight.

I was off the hook. But Kim Myers was next. He had submitted a minority report to the theological committee's very conservative statement, saying that if homosexual persons were able to be baptized and confirmed without a promise of celibacy, they should also be eligible for ordination. He was a forceful speaker, but the bishops were in no mood to consider the logic of a position that rejected a double standard for laity and clergy and affirmed the unity of the sacraments. The bishops who debated his remarks said that he should not license Ellen, and the defense of this position began to take on an inquiry into her personal life. It was astounding to hear bishops of the church openly speculating about what Ellen did or did not do at night behind a closed door. I was livid with the injustice of it all. Kim rose to the point of personal privilege. "Gentlemen," he exploded, "if this conversation continues I am going home and tell Ellen

Barrett to hire a lawyer and sue every damn one of you for libel."

Someone asked Kim if he wanted the House's guidance on licensing Ellen. He said he did not now, although he had hoped for some helpful discussion. Someone called the question, and it was defeated sixty-eight to forty-nine.

Later on in the session the bishops' "pastoral letter" was submitted for discussion. A pastoral letter is a statement from the House of Bishops to the whole Church. It is supposed to be read or circulated in every parish. The letter used the phrase "advocating and/or practicing homosexual" as disqualifying one from ordination. I tried to introduce the qualifier "publicly stated as practicing," to no avail. I felt that without the word "publicly" we would expose our candidates to rumor and our bishops and clergy to an impossible conflict in the use of confidentiality. The letter was voted as written:

PASTORAL LETTER TO THE CHURCH
FROM THE HOUSE OF BISHOPS
October, 1977

From the bishops of the Episcopal Church: greetings and peace in the name of our Lord Jesus Christ.

During our October 1977 meeting we have discovered an encouraging degree of unity among ourselves as we deliberated and prayed together. Since the Minnesota General Convention we have seen some new dimensions incorporated into the life and practice of our Church. For this we rejoice.

We are convinced that canon law is necessary to good order in the Church, but it cannot create unity. The only source of the Church's unity is the Spirit of the Lord Jesus Christ upon whom we wait in trust and patience.

As your fellow Christians we share with you our awareness of the hurt and anger being felt by many members of the Church. We are also aware of greater hurt being experienced by millions throughout the world who are hungry, homeless, dispossessed, powerless and victims of crisis. We have heard you. We have heard them. So we respond.

We have applauded the leadership of our Presiding Bishop in the search for a wider understanding of mission. We commend to this Church our common "Venture in Mission."

The hurt and hunger of body and spirit in the world and in our Church call us to new unity in Christ. He is our Lord and bids us to demonstrate our oneness in him. As your bishops we hold a wide range of views on the problems of the world and of the Church. Yet we experience deep-rooted oneness in Christ.

We call on you to journey with us in faith as we seek to follow our Savior and bring his love to the deep human hurt which all of us feel.

We agree that those who find that they cannot accept the decision to ordain women to the priesthood and episcopacy are nonetheless members in good standing of this Church.

Our present understanding of the Bible and Christian theology makes it inadmissible for this Church to authorize the ordination of anyone who advocates and/or willfully and habitually practices homosexuality.

We are convinced that this Church is to confine its nuptial blessing exclusively to a marriage between a man and a woman.

We urge our Church's increased concern for the crisis in our cities and in our rural areas.

We challenge the members of this Church to accept responsibility for increasing our ecumenical awareness and activity in parishes and dioceses.

We are encouraged that ecumenical conversations reveal a significant converging of theological views among Christians from many traditions.

On the Matter of Conscience

We have sought to recognize that many were dismayed because of General Convention's action concerning the ordination of women, even as others were gladdened and encouraged. No attempt was made to recommend a change in that decision during our meeting. We do affirm that one is not a disloyal Episcopalian if he or she abstains from supporting the decision or continues to be convinced it was an error.

We call for careful avoidance of any kind of pressure which might lead either an advocate or an opponent of the action to offend against his or her conscience. We acknowledge that as bishops we have a special responsibility in this regard. The Minnesota Convention sought to permit but not to coerce. We affirm that no members of the Church should be penalized for conscientious objection to, or support of, the ordination of women. A vivid personal example is the Presiding Bishop himself. He has acknowledged his inability thus far to affirm such ordination. This has dismayed many who rejoice in the admission of women to the priesthood. We nonetheless express our full confidence that he will continue to carry out the duties of his office with integrity. We have made this decision about respect for conscience because we believe it is just. We will continue to reach out to any who might separate from us.

On the Matter of Sexuality

Another issue with which we had to deal was the mysterious and complicated matter of human sexuality. The last General Convention directed this Church to embark upon a study of this important subject in preparation for the next Convention. Nevertheless, under the pressure of questions from Church people the House of Bishops has decided that some statement at this time is needed on the issues of the marriage and the ordination of homosexual persons.

It is clear from Scripture that the sexual union of man and woman is God's will and that this finds holy expression within the covenant of marriage. Therefore this Church confines its nuptial blessing to the union of male and female. It is likewise clear that in ordination, this Church publicly requires each ordinand to fashion his or her personal life after Christ as an example to the faithful. The bishops, therefore, agree to deny ordination to an advocating and/or practicing homosexual person. In each case we must not condone what we believe God wills to redeem.

We are mindful that homosexual persons as children of God have a full and equal claim with all other persons upon the love, acceptance, concern and pastoral care of the Church. Furthermore, they are entitled to equal protection under the law with all other citizens. We call upon our society to see that such protection is provided. We are deeply distressed that in parts of the world such persons are deprived of their civil rights and in some cases are subjected to the tragedy of humiliation, persecution and violence. The Gospel of Jesus Christ compels us to act against these injustices and affirm these persons as our brothers and sisters for whom Christ died.

On the Matter of Mission and Ministry

Our Presiding Bishop has challenged us to "Venture in Mission" as a response to the Gospel. He has issued a clear call for us to join in marshalling the human and financial resources of the people of each diocese in order to bring the joy and healing grace of Christ to the hurts and hungers of the people of the world.

A coalition of urban bishops has directed our attention to the distress of people in cities around the world. We are also mindful of the hardships faced by many in our rural areas. Many of our cities and many of our rural counties are in decay, mirroring the joblessness, poverty and oppression of so many of the people who dwell in them. We are seeking to focus the attention of our Church on an understanding of the root causes of these tragic dislocations of human life and freedom.

Through public hearings and other means, our urban bishops will endeavor to lead the Church into a more responsive ministry, growing out of a more informed strategy for the mission to the urban communities in which many of our people dwell. Strategies are being developed for improved ministry to those in rural areas as, for example, the Navajo Area Mission. We urge all members of our Church to support these efforts with prayer and concern, for these crises are the responsibility of us all.

We are developing new forms of ministry. The bishop in every diocese and the priest in every congregation have long been our usual pattern of ordained ministry. The wider use of the diaconate as a ministry of service, and of the self-supporting ministries is before us. We rejoice that a growing number of lay persons are claiming and exercising their own ministries. Whatever form our ministry takes, each of us is called by God to respond and to seek a deeper understanding of our faith in Christ in order that each may better serve.

As part of Christ's Body, every Episcopalian needs nurturing for that service. It is the obligation of every member to seek a deeper understanding of the Gospel and to pursue training for the particular ministry appropriate to his or her gifts.

In struggling with our differences we have discovered an impressive level of agreement in important areas of faith and discipline. This has brought to us a freedom to face anew our task of mission.

We commend to you the following quotation from the 1968 Lambeth Conference:

"Our message is a message of hope. God is active in his world. The changes which bewilder are not all evil, though all challenge us to find the right human response. God is active in His Church, renewing it so that the Church may more fully proclaim its faith to the world, more effectively discharge its mission of service to the world, and may recover that unity for which our Lord prayed and without which it cannot be truly itself. It is for us to recognize the signs of his renewing action and to welcome them and obey them. It is no time for either despair or doubt.

Rather it is a time to remember the Lord's saying: 'Be of good cheer: I have overcome the world.' "

Your bishops believe that the great days of the Church are not just in the past but in the present and in the future.

A young man who was reporting on the meeting for Integrity asked to see me during the last days of the meeting. He was hurt and felt betrayed by what had gone on. Although I had avoided censure and felt relieved, especially because of the effect it would have on my diocesan convention three weeks away, I was also depressed. I knew why my colleagues felt as they did. I knew the pressure they were under. But I still felt that they might have had more sympathy for the human element in the debate, and been more motivated to befriend and support a persecuted minority of faithful churchmen. I was just as convinced then as I am now that the homosexual community's persecution should have commanded more sympathy than the hurt feelings of those who had left the Church over women's ordination and the new Prayer Book.

Along the pathways of the immaculately groomed Sandpiper Inn, there were "Beware of the Alligators" signs posted along the approach to the water. The former Bishop of Alaska played golf between sessions, and one day he sliced a drive into the lagoon. As he leaned over to coax his ball within reach, a large alligator rose up and consumed it. We heard later that alligators have a passion for marshmallows and often mistake golf balls for this delicacy. Later in the week the local newspaper had a story about a man who was peacefully tending his garden when a hungry alligator "grabbed him by the leg and attempted to drag him into a canal." Such is life in a motel in Florida. I was so glad to get back to the safety of the streets of Morningside Heights.

13

Away from the Alligators

I was glad to get back to New York, away from the alligators, away from the anxiety of the House of Bishops. This was my town. Driving home from the airport over the Triborough Bridge, all of Manhattan spread out before me In the distance on the left was the skyline. Over the great old buildings stood the two new towers of the World Trade Center. I recalled the joy of the crowds during the Bicentennial celebration surging down to the Battery to watch the tall ships, and I remembered the sermon I preached in the midst of it all at old Trinity. My sight moved up the East River to the midtown skyscrapers. The United Nations, clean and white on the river, the old Empire State still the tallest building there, the Chrysler Building with its glistening Art Deco pinnacle. We have churches spread throughout this part of town, and I thought about each one.

We crossed the Triborough bridge and drove across 125th Street. Harlem. Most people in New York do not see it if they do not live there. I not only live on its edge, but I frequently pass through on visits to the ghetto for church services and meetings. Almost every day I see the shocking numbers of unemployed young people on the corners, the winos, hookers, pimps, hustlers, cops, the Cadillacs, burnt-out buildings, and rip-off stores. This is the rhythm of Harlem, even harsher than the streets described by James Baldwin and Langston Hughes. The music blaring forth is angry, not the smooth tones of Duke Ellington. Harlem has produced great artists who have changed the soul of America. But Harlem is also the anger and shame of our land. Within three blocks of one of our churches is a street corner where more heroin changes hands than anywhere in the world.

Our little battles over homosexuality seemed a long way from what I was seeing on the drive home from LaGuardia. My own convention was to occur in ten days. My life seemed out of touch, just one damn convention after another. This one, however, was really important, and my anxiety grew. The day I came home, I had a funeral for an old black priest who had ministered humbly and with courage for over fifty years. Sunday was full. Harlem in the morning, old Southern Baptist hymns and elaborate Anglo-Catholic ritual. A major sermon at the cathedral that afternoon as we installed the new canons. That evening, in a tiny parish on West 126th Street, I recognized the orders of Emily Hewitt, the last of the Philadelphia ordinands. That same week I instituted a young priest in Staten Island, and confirmed some children at a school for troubled youngsters which we run in the northern part of the diocese.

In between these various events I was hearing rumors about the coming convention. I was worried sick. I would wake up in the early morning and go through all the possibilities of what might happen. I wondered again whether Ellen's ordination had been the right thing to do. Should I resign? I rewrote and rewrote my convention address. At home I was either irritable or preoccupied. Phone calls and personal conversations momentarily reassured me, and then I'd panic. All that I had tried to do over the years in the diocese could be ripped apart by this convention. The confidence to continue our work in the city, the unity needed to keep the northern part of the diocese together, the easy relationship I had with most of the clergy; all this could begin to disintegrate if lines were drawn and angry words said which could never be recalled. I was in a dilemma. Some said I should back down and agree not to ordain any homosexual until the national Church made a statement at its next convention. Others said ignore it, that people were sick and tired of the issue. Some black clergy thought of it as another attempt to avoid the real issues of racism in the Church and in the world. Gay people called on me to take a strong stand.

Convention day arrived. At 9:30 A.M. precisely, I put on my crimson academic gown and walked into the convention hall. About seven hundred clergy and lay delegates from all over the diocese were milling around talking to each other. I called the convention to order and we sang a hymn celebrating unity:

> In Christ there is no East nor West
> In him no South or North,
> But one great fellowship of love
> Throughout the whole wide earth.

Would it were so, I thought to myself. After saying a prayer, I rapped the table with the traditional antique gavel.

Once the convention was actually in process, I began to have a good time. Chairing one is like running the rapids in a canoe. You have a sense of speed, of onrushing events. You never know when you will suddenly be confronted with a jagged rock. The canoe tips, then rights itself and continues along. I suppose I enjoy the momentary sense of power and control. But I also like to see representatives from everywhere and every perspective sitting together in one room. I have gotten to know so many of them. I know their parishes and sometimes their personal problems. I can even anticipate which side of a question they will take, and whether they will be angry, or funny, or exasperatingly intellectual. I have never had a bad convention, despite all my fears, but this one was more perilous than any. After a quorum was an-

nounced, I fingered the pages of the address I was about
to give and on which so much would depend.

ADDRESS TO THE CONVENTION OF THE DIOCESE OF NEW YORK
October 18, 1977

Life is a mystery. Each day, each week, opens up new events
to be untangled, deciphered, somehow ordered. Like Sisyphus,
we push the stone of understanding up the mountain of confusion;
for a moment see clear the view of the world as a whole, only to
be tripped up and have the rock come tumbling down, tripped
up by a small happening in our personal life—a broken relationship,
a betrayal, struck down by a death; struck down by a catastrophe
of history. We lie panting at the bottom of the mountain, we look
around, we pray for grace and courage to begin once more the
task of making sense out of it all.

For a Christian, the gospel is both a confusing and a clarifying
instrument for this purpose. You kneel before the image of Christ
on the Cross and pain begins to make sense. You stand alone in
the Holy Sepulcher deep in the great rock of Jerusalem—still standing after all those years of historic destruction—and you feel a
power rising out of its very darkness. The power is not yours,
depends not upon your muddled mind, rises and lets fall independent of your tiny being. And yet the power is in you, too, and
you feel part of it and part of the rock. Yes, the gospel makes
enormous sense on a level of being beyond sense. On this level,
the gospel reveals a deeper truth than any reasoned analysis. This
is the gospel of Faith, the gospel that puts a King on the Cross,
drops wisdom from the mouth of a clown or a child, and lifts up
the riches of a poor widow far beyond the riches of a prince. This
is the gospel of the heart, the gospel you can feed upon in the
innermost spirit. And you can feed upon it because it blows glory
into the deepest humiliation and lets flow the waters of forgiveness
into the most dried-up sinful being. You need this gospel to survive
in the desert of life. You need its light to travel in the darkness.

However, because it has this power to rescue us out of the deepest
abyss, it is the same gospel which brings down the wisdom of the
just and confounds the judges and philosophers in their conclusions. Its power cannot be contained within the neat theorems of
psychiatrists or theologians any more than God can be contained
within a brass box set upon the altar.

Thus, the paradox of gospel mixed with the continual surprise
of life and history makes the unfolding of the Christian faith continually exciting. In lighting the most elemental mysteries of life, the
Word excites men even to give their lives for it or rather, to give

their lives for Him who spoke it and lived it.

However mysterious and seemingly contradictory the gospel, however beyond reason, our tradition insists it is never *contrary* to reason. Therefore, with mind as well as with confident heart we continue to push the God-given rock of understanding up the mountain of confusion as best we can. We believe the words of Jesus that the Holy Spirit continually reveals new truth. But new truth is difficult to see as truth because it makes old truth seem less than true. Furthermore, what seems new truth often is found to be less than true, to be a tempting aberration from gospel. To these doubtful new truths we apply Gamaliel's law: "Let these men alone; for if this plan or undertaking is of men, it will fail; but if it is of God, you will not be able to overthrow them. You might even be found opposing God!" (Acts 5:38)

In the meantime, however, some resist the real new truth while others embrace it and push its implications to the limit. In just such a situation we now find ourselves.

Some feel that the modern revolution in sexuality contains a freer way of living out the Commandment of love, a way more consistent than ever before with the gospel of incarnate love. This incarnation first made it possible to sanctify the responsible long-ings of the flesh, for He Himself took on flesh. Others feel that this new understanding is of the devil and threatens the very foun-dation of discipline and order on which the Church is built. Some see the world, created by God in all its variety, to be a source of revelation for the Church. Indeed, Jesus was wont to point to a Samaritan or a Roman centurion, who lived in the world outside the Church, as an image bearer for the Kingdom. Others see the world as a threat to the Church, see the Church standing pure against the world. Did not Jesus say, "I have overcome the world"? Has not the world always led to the downfall of the Christian? Some see the words of the New Testament as totally inviolate, equal in importance and authority. Others see these words as condi-tioned by the cultural context in which they were spoken and give them a priority of value under the higher law of the Word himself, the law of love.

I have wrestled long and hard with these questions, especially as they apply to the ordination of one who has publicly admitted her homosexual orientation. I still believe we did the right thing. I believe that this ordinand's ministry will prove to be a worthy vessel for the priesthood. I am sorry, however, that whether such a person should be ordained became the occasion for this discus-sion, because the Church's accepting a vocation to the ministry is a highly personal and pastoral matter. Remember, we did not ordain a class of persons, but an individual. Moreover, in the paradox of gospel the very condition which caused this controversy may prove to be the handicap through which the power of Christ will shine.

I do not plan today to offer another rationale for our action in this ordination. You have read my thoughts on the subject. However, I would like to clarify our action once more.

In reading over the hundreds of letters I received, I sense that many people in the Church are upset because they feel we gave a blessing to the practice of homosexuality. We did no such thing. The ordinand's admitted psychological *orientation* was the only issue considered. The policy of the diocese in this ordination did not involve considering the ordination of a publicly avowed *practicing* homosexual person. Alleged quotations to this effect on the part of Ellen Barrett, whether true or false, came to light after her ordination.

But to say that we believe the ordination of one individual was right is not to say that I have by any means worked through the problems of sexual morality in this new age. I am still pushing the stone of understanding up the mountain of confusion.

I believe sexuality to be a mysterious gift by which we are led to love one another. It also is a gift by which men and women are made different and through the exercise of which new persons are brought into the world. Sexuality, the psychologists teach us, invades all our affective lives, all our desires and emotions of love. Its power, some believe, is the same power from which our longings for God Himself come forth. Tradition uses the love song of the Song of Solomon as a paradigm of Christ's love for the Church.

I personally feel that the day may come soon when a responsible homosexual relationship will be seen as not contrary to God's will. However, at this point in time, an official statement or action to that effect would be premature and inappropriate.

Since all of us are still far from understanding the mysteries of personality and of theology, it is most important that every part of the Church continue to study, to talk and to pray that we find God's will. The General Convention has requested a study, and the House of Bishops has asked each diocese to appoint a commission to study human sexuality and the Church. I am, therefore, appointing a Diocesan Commission to study these matters and to hold hearings whereby all responsible points of view within the diocese may be heard. I will ask them to report their findings to the next year's convention, so that our conclusions on these matters may be more informed.

As you will hear in the Pastoral Letter from the House of Bishops, the whole Church has been wrestling with this problem. I was gratified that the House of Bishops, having heard the facts, did not deplore the ordination of Ellen Barrett. Let me share part of my address to them when a resolution deploring the ordination of Ellen Barrett was on the floor.

I then quoted my address to the House of Bishops, ending with the paragraph:

"If this action is formally disapproved, my brothers, I will feel that this House and I differ radically about what the meaning of the apostolic office of Bishop really is. Is it to manage, administer, and keep safe a steadily decreasing number of frightened and confused people; or is it to see the modern world as it is, and bring to that changing, suffering world the liberating, loving message of the Gospel of Christ."

The House of Bishops' conclusion at this session is in line with the present policy of our diocese and would allow a qualified person of homosexual orientation to be ordained. However, they are not willing at this time to go further. Thus it is my present policy also to await the findings of the Commission before considering the ordination of a publicly avowed, practicing homosexual, or one who would advocate the same. This, as I say, is in line with the conclusion reached at the House of Bishops meeting.

Let me reiterate, we are dealing with a most complex problem. It includes the issues of the authority of the Church, the authority of Scripture, the nature of the Bishop's office, the doctrine of sacrament, the theology of ordination, the nature of man, the place of psychiatric theory in the Church, the relation of the Church to the world, the dynamics of sexuality, the interpretation of church history, and the role of the standing committees, to name a few.

This is a most delicate issue. Literally thousands of Episcopalians have been hurt and confused by the ordination and by the misunderstanding surrounding it—even to the point of leaving the Church. For this I am deeply sorry. I hate to hurt anyone, particularly those for whom I have pastoral responsibility, particularly those I love.

This ordination has been called a scandal in the life of the Church. However, the Church is guilty of an even more serious scandal, a more violent offense against charity, in its treatment of homosexual persons. The very nickname "faggot" derives from the sticks used to burn allegedly homosexual persons at the stake. The priest to whom I owe the most, who pointed me toward the ministry, was literally destroyed by the Church's cruel treatment because of his homosexuality. I know many gay people who have left the Church wounded. I know many who, because of their deep love for Christ, have stayed in the Church despite the misunderstanding and persecution. We also are all aware of the harsh discrimination against homosexual persons in the secular world.

I am concerned today that we not offend either group further by impulsive anger or uncharitable debate. I also do not see how, in a short hour or so on convention floor, the mind of the Church can possibly be expressed in such a complex matter. Believe me, my friends, no simple answer to the question exists. I hope, therefore, that if there is debate it will be measured and dignified, in accordance with the fine tradition of this convention. I also hope that you will await the findings of the Commission, as I plan to do, before making up your mind, before passing any final resolutions.

In any case, I will not consider views for or against as reflecting upon the Bishop of New York personally, I assure you.

The House of Bishops affirmed once more the belief that Anglicans of very different views can live together in the same church, that what binds us together is far stronger than what separates us. Even more important, we have been called by our Saviour to bring love and hope and strength to our communities which are in such desperate need. Nothing must interfere with this mission.

I then spoke of some internal problems of the diocese and concluded as follows:

Although I am basically optimistic about the life of our Church, I am deeply troubled by the signs of death in all of our urban areas, from Poughkeepsie* to Staten Island. Arson and unemployment increase. Crime abounds. Prisoners rot. Children are undernourished in mind, body and soul. The great agony of the black and Spanish ghetto and the suffering of poor elderly people continues in silence and invisibility. Our inner-city parishes minister in the jungle of despair. Our efforts, though successful, are a tiny spark in the darkness. Pray, my friends, that the great strength, the great heart of America, will soon turn its attention to these abandoned places. I hope the President's visit to the South Bronx will be a turning point in national policy.

In closing, let me say:

My experience at the House of Bishops this last week had a great effect on me. *I am so happy to be home!* I am so happy to be bishop of this wonderful, crazy, diverse, vital, exciting diocese. Last

---

* Since this book has gone to press, we have learned that one of our small parishes in Poughkeepsie, New York, has left the Episcopal Church.

week I had a special-delivery letter from a lady who had misread the report of Bishop Allin's suggested resignation in the *New York Times*. She thought that I had offered to resign. *No way!*

At this point I was interrupted by applause, which grew louder and turned into a standing ovation. Tears came to my eyes, relief flooded through my being. Everything would be all right. I was caught by surprise. I had no idea this would happen, especially this year. When the applause subsided, I concluded:

I love all of you. I love New York. I have the best job in the country. And I know this is the greatest diocese in the Church.

When we reconvened after lunch, we went into a committee of the whole with Bishop Wetmore presiding. All resolutions having to do with sexuality would now be heard:

16. *Resolved:* that the Bishops and Standing Committee of the Diocese of New York hereby cease and desist from ordaining, or recommending for ordination, to either the Diaconate or the Priesthood all persons who admit to homosexual orientation as their chief sexual expression, at least until such time as the Church has studied, reported on, and taken action on human sexuality in General Convention.

17. *Therefore be it resolved:* that the Convention of the Diocese of New York recommends to its Bishops, Standing Committee and Ministries Commission that no criteria of ordination to the sacred ministry be adopted which would establish a different standard of morality for clergy than that which applies to all Christians or which would force any candidate for holy orders as a condition for ordination to repudiate aspects of emotional or sexual orientation which such candidate believes to be valid and honorable reflections of God's love.

18. *And be it further resolved:* that this Convention appoint a commission to study questions concerning sexual orientation and expression as they relate to membership and ministry in the Church, and report their findings and recommendations to the 1978 Convention.

[From the Rev. Thomas W. Bauer]

19. *Be it resolved:* that this 199th Convention of the Diocese of New York reaffirms that the only practice of sexual activity that is blessed and legitimized by our Lord Jesus Christ (as attested in Holy Scripture and set forth in the Book of Common Prayer) is that between a man and a woman who are committed to one another in the bond of marriage.

[From the Rev. C. FitSimons Allison,
the Rev. Norman J. Catir, Jr.]

Bishop Wetmore is a good presiding officer. He opened by calmly stating why we were in special session and the rules which would govern it. There would be, he said, an opportunity for any representative of a group of persons to speak for five minutes. All individual speakers were limited to three minutes. The total time to be given was one hour. No new arguments appeared that afternoon, and I was not surprised by the range of points of view I heard. It seemed to me that the balance of speakers was wholesome and the level of debate respectable. One speaker went a little off color and the convention wanted to laugh but stifled it. A lay person told a painful story about her son who was seduced by a priest many years before. Theological scholars, progressive and conservative, quoted from Scripture to support their respective arguments on homosexuality. A psychiatrist gave a brief professional view. My anxiety lessened as the debate proceeded. It was going to be all right. We were going to get through the day. About five minutes before the end of the debate, a priest moved that all resolutions having to do with homosexuality be referred to a commission on sexuality which I was to appoint.

The resolution referring the questions on sexuality to a commission passed. The debate was over. When the convention adjourned, I knew that a spirit of reconciliation had prevailed. I had a few good phone calls that night. Since then, the issue has calmed down. We will await the findings of the diocesan commission in the fall of 1978.

I am still not satisfied with the situation we now face within the life of the Church. The scars are very deep. I know many clergy and lay people who will never really trust the Church again. I know some who have left the Church and will never return. One parish still withholds its assessment. Others have decided to pay but have no great enthusiasm for the work we do together. Homosexual persons were deeply offended by the Pastoral Letter of the House of Bishops. Some of them, who seek ordination, are deathly afraid of what may come out of the next diocesan convention, but more especially from the General Convention in the fall of 1979. An uneasy peace has settled over the homosexual issue.

The movement for a separated "schismatic church" gains momentum. It is said that they will soon consecrate their own bishop, that the three bishops necessary for such a consecration have been lined up.* I gather that about thirty parishes have left our Church and that others are considering it. I do not think that this number will increase appreciably. Where the parishes have left, lawsuits for the property are proceeding in some dioceses. Whether a schismatic parish can keep its property and endowment has to be fought out in court and the outcome largely depends on the laws of the particular state. Although I voted for it, I am bothered by the so-called conscience clause passed by the House of Bishops, because it virtually allows anyone to break the canons or differ from the doctrine and discipline of the Church so long as he states he does it out of conscience.

Such goings-on are painful for a church. I feel badly, very badly, to have been even a small part of the cause. And yet there was the issue, clear and insistent. Does candor, openness, honesty about one's sexuality, bar someone from ordination? If I had the decision to make again, I am sure

---

* One retired Episcopal bishop and one bishop of the Philipino Independent Church conducted a service to consecrate bishops in a schismatic church. The Anglican Church of North America is established but claims few members.

my answer would be the same. Most important of all, the thousands of homosexual persons who have been persecuted by society and denigrated by the Church have seen a sign of hope.

Meanwhile Brenda, Patience, my sixteen-year-old daughter, and I live happily on in the J. P. Morgan château on the heights overlooking Harlem. My other eight children and their children come by from time to time. I still feel I have the most wonderful job in the world, being part of the great swirl of events that shape the city, the country, and the Church, to be able to help a little here and there, to be allowed to share the most intimate parts of people's lives. I thrive on the excitement of this city, the feeling of living on the brink of totally unforeseeable happenings. Over it all, I have a sense of God's presence, a feeling that although I may make mistakes, still He is guiding me in the general direction I should go. The controversies over women's ordination and homosexuality are not over, but I feel that we still have the flexibility for building a more compassionate Church so that our image will more closely resemble the image of Christ, and the allegiance of all of God's people, in all their diversity, will grow stronger.

Epilogue

I am still studying, thinking, talking, praying about the proper course for myself. Time and again, I am torn between what I personally think or feel and what appear to be the demands of my office. For instance, I wanted to ordain women to the priesthood long before the Philadelphia ordination, yet I felt bound by the canons of the Church and by a responsibility to those who were opposed. I have to be a bishop to the whole Church, not just to those who agree with me. I also felt that the Church did need more time to get used to the idea of women clergy. It seemed wiser then, looking to the long-range goal of having women accepted as ministers, to wait for General Convention action. In retrospect, however, it seems doubtful that the convention would have acted positively had it not been for the Philadelphia ordination and the vigorous discussion it aroused. Could it be that they were right in going forward with the ordination, and that I was right in holding back?

The last several months have been quiet. I receive only occasional letters on the issues which once were so volatile. Only one of our parishes, as of September 1978, is still withholding its assessment. Some say they were assured by the pastoral letter from the House of Bishops; others say they have made their protest and are now willing to be a part of the mission of the Church, though they still disagree with their bishop. A comparative peace reigns within the Diocese of New York. I have not forced anyone to participate in a Eucharist celebrated by a woman, nor have any publicly acknowledged homosexuals applied for ordination. A diocesan study commission on sexuality continues to meet around the diocese, but their hearings draw very few participants. The Church is fairly calm, and I am thankful for this.

But reaction against homosexuality grows in other places. Minneapolis–St. Paul, a fairly liberal community, followed Miami in voting against gay rights legislation. I am fearful that other municipalities will do the same. I cannot help feeling that anti-gay legislation is a retrogressive movement. Yet it may only be of brief duration. So often movements are set back after their initial impact, but then, if their cause is just, surge forward after a time.

I am still studying, thinking, and praying about the morality of sexuality and have by no means reached conclusions. However, my own personal thinking at the present time is leaning toward the view that sexual activity between consenting adults outside marriage is not *per se* sinful. As with any human activity, it can be sinful and sick, or generous and loving. It is time for ancient taboos to be lifted so that the moral reality of sexual relations can be seen clearly.

I cannot believe that two lonely people comforting one another with physical love is necessarily sinful, even if they are not married. I cannot believe that a husband forcing his wife into sexual intercourse against her will is without sin.

In the present day few are privileged to have a loving sexual relationship in marriage. Is sexual love therefore reserved only for that small group of persons, when it is so important a part of the human personality, when it is psychologically tied so closely to loving our neighbors and our God? I find it hard to equate my understanding of Christ's love and justice with such a position.

Sexuality is powerful, beautiful, God-given. Let not fear,

anger, prejudice, superstition, and taboo determine our understanding of it. Rather let the light of the intellect, the wisdom of all ages, the compassion of a merciful Saviour, and the common sense of daily living guide our judgment. Many suffer today because of their sexuality. Many are finding courage to express a new morality of grace and love. May their sacrifice bring to future generations a deeper humanity, a fuller charity, and a greater opportunity to follow Him who knew the heart of the gospel to be love.

Since this manuscript was finished, the Lambeth Conference, a conference of Anglican bishops from all over the world that convenes every ten years, has taken place in England. This year 430 bishops attended. Although Lambeth has no jurisdiction over the member national churches, the bishops' consensus has great influence on the general direction of our Church. Meeting at Canterbury, the official seat of the Archbishop of Canterbury, who is the presiding officer and "first amongst equals" of our communion, we passed two resolutions of interest to this book.

One resolution noted the ordination of women to the priesthood of the "Catholic and Apostolic ministry." It encouraged the Provinces (member churches) who have not ordained women to discuss the matter with those who had, and when appropriate, to invite ordained women to function as priests within their churches. The implication of the resolution was that women could and indeed had been ordained. Further, the freedom of conscience to hold different views while maintaining our unity was affirmed as essential to the genius of Anglicanism.

The other resolution was a brief statement on homosexuality:

While we reaffirm heterosexuality as a scriptural norm, we recognize the need for deep and dispassionate study of the question of homosexuality, which would take seriously both the teaching of scripture and the results of scientific and medical research. The Church, recognizing the need for pastoral concern for those who are homosexual, encourages dialogue with them.

This seemingly innocuous statement is important. It states the existence of this issue in the Church, and although offering heterosexuality as the biblical norm, it does not condemn homosexuality. Further, it encourages the study of this phenomenon to include dialogue with homosexual persons. I trust that such sense and constraint will inform our own next General Convention in the Episcopal Church of the United States.

Women are priests in our Church, but women priests are far from being considered for positions on an equal basis with male priests. I believe it is the duty of every Christian to search out prejudices within himself or herself, and within the Church at large, so that women will be able to have equal opportunity within the family of God.

We are even further behind in understanding and accepting homosexuality. Scientists do not agree on its etiology. Moralists do not agree on its morality. Christians do not agree about its relative sinfulness, and most people still are filled with anxiety or anger concerning the subject.

I have written this book because I believe the issues of sexuality are urgent. We can no longer afford cheap locker room humor about "broads" and "queers." We can no longer communicate to younger people by quoting old rules at them. Rather, let us get on with an understanding of the holy gift of sexuality appropriate for our time.

Index